Quick Guide

S H E D S

CREATIVE HOMEOWNER PRESS®

Writer: Jim Barrett.
Illustrator: Mario Ferro
Book Packager: Boultinghouse & Boultinghouse, Inc.

Cover Design: Warren Ramezzana
Cover Illustrations: Moffit Cecil

Electronic Prepress: TSI Graphics
Printed at: Quebecor Printing Inc.

Vinyl siding drawing courtesy of Certainteed Corp.

Current Printing (last digit)
10 9 8 7 6 5 4 3

Quick Guide: Storage Sheds
LC: 93-71658
ISBN: 1-880029-20-0 (paper)

CREATIVE HOMEOWNER PRESS®
A Division of Federal Marketing Corp.
24 Park Way
Upper Saddle River, NJ 07458

C O N T E N T S

S A F E T Y   F I R S T

Although all the designs and methods in this book have been tested for safety, it is not possible to overstate the importance of using the safest methods possible. What follows are reminders; some do's and don'ts. They are not substitutes for your own common sense. Always use caution, care, and good judgment when following the procedures described in this book.

■ *Always* be sure that the electrical setup is safe; be sure that no circuit is overloaded, and that all power tools and electrical outlets are properly grounded. Do not use power tools in wet locations.

■ *Always* read container labels on paints, solvents, and other products; provide ventilation, and observe all other warnings.

■ *Always* read the tool manufacturer's instructions for using a tool, especially the warnings.

■ *Always* use holders or pushers to work pieces shorter or more narrow than 3 inches on a table saw or jointer. Avoid working short pieces if you can.

■ *Always* remove the key from any drill chuck (portable or press) before starting the drill.

■ *Always* pay deliberate attention to how a tool works so that you can avoid being injured.

■ *Always* know the limitations of your tools. Do not try to force them to do what they were not designed to do.

■ *Always* make sure that any adjustment is locked before proceeding. For example, always check the rip fence on a table saw or the bevel adjustment on a portable saw before starting to work.

■ *Always* clamp small pieces firmly to a bench or other work surfaces when sawing or drilling.

■ *Always* wear the appropriate rubber or work gloves when handling chemicals, heavy construction or when sanding.

■ *Always* wear a disposable mask when working with odors, dusts or mists. Use a special respirator when working with toxic substances.

■ *Always* wear eye protection, especially when using power tools or striking metal on metal or concrete; a chip can fly off, for example, when chiseling concrete.

■ *Always* be aware that there is never time for your body's reflexes to save you from injury from a power tool in a dangerous situation; everything happens too fast. Be *alert!*

■ *Always* keep your hands away from the business ends of blades, cutters and bits.

■ *Always* use a drill with an auxiliary handle to control the torque when large size bits are used.

■ *Always* check your local building codes when planning new construction. The codes are intended to protect public safety and should be observed to the letter.

■ *Never* work with power tools when you are tired or under the influence of alcohol or drugs.

■ *Never* cut very small pieces of wood or pipe. Only cut pieces that are large enough to hold or clamp securely in place.

■ *Never* change a blade or a bit unless the power cord is unplugged. Do not depend on the switch being off; you might accidentally hit it.

■ *Never* work in insufficient lighting.

■ *Never* work while wearing loose clothing, hanging hair, open cuffs, or jewelry.

■ *Never* work with dull tools. Have them sharpened, or learn how to sharpen them yourself.

■ *Never* use a power tool on a workpiece that is not firmly supported or clamped.

■ *Never* saw a workpiece that spans a large distance between horses without close support on both sides of the kerf; the piece can bend, closing the kerf and jamming the blade, causing saw kickback.

■ *Never* support a workpiece with your leg or other part of your body when sawing.

■ *Never* carry sharp or pointed tools, such as utility knives, awls, or chisels in your pocket. If you want to carry tools, use a special-purpose tool belt with leather pockets and holders.

DESIGNING YOUR SHED

The size, shape, and architectural design of the shed will depend largely on what you plan to use it for, or what you intend to store in it. This chapter covers basic design considerations and discusses four popular shed designs.

Design Elements

Depending on what you intend to use your shed for, you may call it a tool or utility shed, woodshed, garden shed, or simply a general-purpose storage shed. The intended use of the shed will also determine its location on the property, its basic architectural style, and the architectural details you incorporate into it. For example, a large shed designed to house wheeled equipment may require wide, double barn-style doors and a ramp leading to the opening. If the shed will double as a small workshop or other workspace, you may want to add one or more windows, lights and electrical outlets, interior wall coverings (wallboard or paneling), and even a utility sink. In a small shed used strictly for storage, you may not want to include windows at all, to maximize interior wall space for shelving or hanging items. In a larger shed, you might install a skylight in the roof to increase wall space.

This book focuses on outdoor storage sheds up to about 120 square feet. It does not provide details for large workshops, animal shelters, small barns, summer houses, poolside structures, or similar outbuildings. However, you can use many of the basic construction techniques to build practically any size or type of outbuilding you want, then modify it to suit your needs.

Shed Kits. If you don't want to build your shed from scratch, look for shed kits at lumberyards and home centers. These include the lumber and other materials precut to exact sizes. All you do is assemble the pieces (nails and other hardware may or may not be included), following the instructions that come with the kit.

Roof Styles

Architecturally, sheds are usually classified by roof design. This book provides plans for building three popular shed styles: a shed-roof shed, a

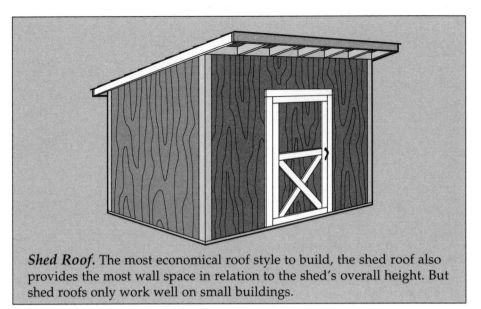

Shed Roof. The most economical roof style to build, the shed roof also provides the most wall space in relation to the shed's overall height. But shed roofs only work well on small buildings.

gable-roof shed, and a barn-style shed. In addition, you'll find plans for building a lean-to shed that can be attached to an exterior wall of your house, a tall fence, or a garden wall.

Shed Roof

This roof style is the simplest and most economical to build. It consists of a single slope from a taller front wall to a shorter back wall. A shed roof provides the most wall storage space in relation to the overall height of the building, making it practical where a low-profile roof is desired or building codes restrict overall shed height. A shed-roof design is also the most practical when you're building a lean-to shed against the house or a garden wall. On such sheds, the roof usually slants away from the house wall. Whether the shed is freestanding or lean-to, the entire front wall may be omitted to provide maximum light and access, such as for housing bicycles, garden tools and equipment, firewood, and other items that don't require complete weather protection.

However, a shed-roof design is usually suitable only for small or narrow sheds (6 to 8 feet wide) because the rafters must span the entire width of the roof. Also, the relatively low roof pitch may not be suitable in climates

where the roof will be subjected to heavy snow loads during the winter. On low sheds, access is typically limited to the front (tall) side.

Gable Roof

Although a bit harder to frame than a shed roof, gable roofs are often chosen for their simplicity of design and adaptability to a variety of building sizes, architectural styles, and climatic conditions. They consist of two equal roof pitches that meet at a center ridgeline. Conventional framing consists of individual rafters attached to a center ridge board at the roof peak; the roof pitch determines how much overhead storage is available and how well the roof will shed rain and snow. Access doors may be located on any of the four walls, provided the side walls are tall enough to provide adequate overhead clearance.

An alternative to conventional roof framing on larger sheds is to buy prefabricated roof trusses. Prefab trusses simplify the roof-framing procedure, but they come in limited roof pitches and spans, and the truss members interfere with overhead storage. For more on installing trusses for gable roofs, see pages 44–45.

Barn-Style Roof

This style, also known as a gambrel roof, is popular in rural settings. Barn roofs provide more headroom and overhead storage than shed or gable roofs, but the framing is more complicated. These roofs have two pitches, usually about 30 degrees for the top members and 60 degrees for the bottom members. Rather than framing the rafters individually, you preassemble the rafter members into trusses, then attach each truss assembly to the walls. For smaller backyard sheds, you can assemble complete framing units, called ribs, which consist of the roof members, wall studs, and in some cases, floor joists. The latter method is often used for small barn-style shed kits in which all of the framing members are precut to exact sizes and angles. Both methods are described on pages 46 and 56–58. If the side walls are tall enough, you can locate the access doors in any of the four walls of a barn-style shed; in most cases, however, the door will go in one of the end walls. On large barn-style sheds, double barn doors are often used to provide access for large equipment.

Lean-To Sheds

As mentioned, most lean-to sheds have a shed-roof design, although other roof styles are possible. When attaching a shed to the house, you'll probably want to match the roofing and siding materials to those of the main structure.

Typically, the exterior wall of the house, (or one face of the fence or garden wall) serves as the back wall of the shed. Ledgers are attached to the house wall to support the roof framing, shed side walls, and floor. For more on lean-to shed construction, see pages 50–53.

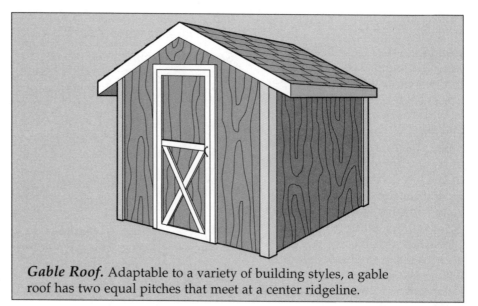

Gable Roof. Adaptable to a variety of building styles, a gable roof has two equal pitches that meet at a center ridgeline.

Barn-style Roof. Also called a gambrel roof, this style provides lots of storage and headroom. But it is more complicated to build than other styles.

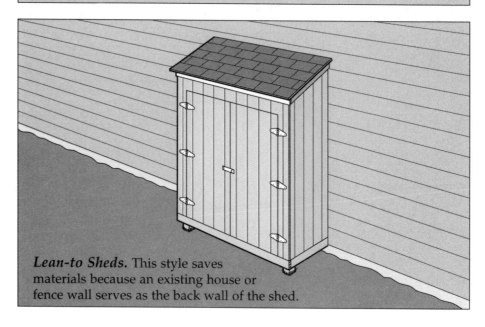

Lean-to Sheds. This style saves materials because an existing house or fence wall serves as the back wall of the shed.

Other Design Features

Beyond the basic four designs shown on pages 6–7, the finished appearance of the shed will depend largely on the type of exterior materials and details you incorporate into the structure: roofing and siding materials, doors, windows, exterior trim, and paint. If budget allows, you can design the shed to match the architectural style of the main house by using the same type of roofing, siding, and trim materials, matching the roof style and pitch, and so on. Even a simple utility shed with plywood siding can be spruced up with trim and moldings. Take a look at other sheds and outbuildings in your neighborhood for ideas.

Windows and Doors. Operating windows provide both light and ventilation. They can be positioned to take advantage of summer breezes; double-insulated windows can provide solar heat gain during the winter months. The size of the shed door depends largely on shed use: make sure the entry door is wide enough to easily accommodate the largest piece of equipment you expect to store in the shed. Also consider how the size

and placement of doors and windows will affect wall storage inside.

Steps and Ramps. The type of foundation you choose for the shed (pages 14–15) will determine the finished floor height. This, in turn, determines whether you'll need to install a ramp or step-up to the entrance. If the shed floor is higher than 10 inches above ground level, add a step or small platform at the entry; because sheds are typically built without crawl spaces beneath, no more than one step should be needed. If the shed floor is 6 inches or higher, you may want to build a short entry ramp of wood or poured concrete to provide easy access for wheeled garden equipment and hand trucks.

Wiring. If you want electrical service in the shed, you'll need to plan a route for the wires or conduit between the shed and house. If you simply want to install a light fixture or two, you can probably tap into a convenient junction box in the house or garage without overloading the circuit. If, on the other hand, you want to install one or more outlets for operating power tools or other high-

amperage equipment, it's best to provide a separate circuit for them. Consult an electrician.

Ventilation. Even if the shed has an operating window, you may need to provide additional ventilation to keep the interior relatively cool and dry during hot or humid weather. Depending on the use your shed is designed for, you may want to install screened eaves vents or gable vents (the screens keep out insects, birds, and small animals). If you want to get fancy, install a cupola on the roof peak of a gable-roof or barn-style shed to serve the same purpose. All of these vents are placed at or near the top of the building: as hot air rises, it escapes through the vents, pulling cooler air through open windows or the gap under the shed door at floor level. If the shed has no window, you may want to install a wall vent at floor level. If possible, place the vents to take advantage of summer breezes to provide cross-ventilation. If the shed will have a concrete perimeter foundation or exterior wood skirting between the floor and ground level, you'll also need to install foundation vents. See the facing page for these venting options.

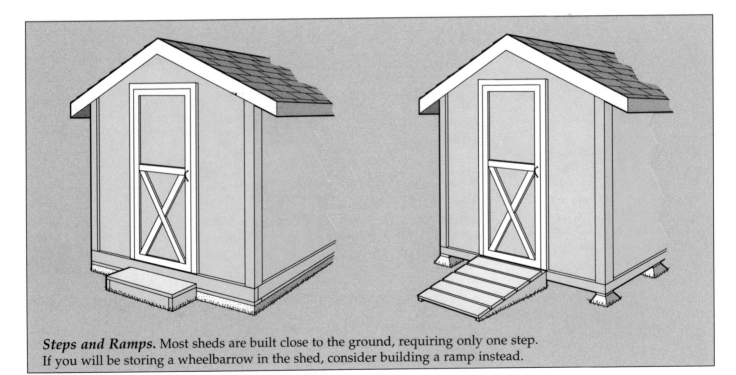

Steps and Ramps. Most sheds are built close to the ground, requiring only one step. If you will be storing a wheelbarrow in the shed, consider building a ramp instead.

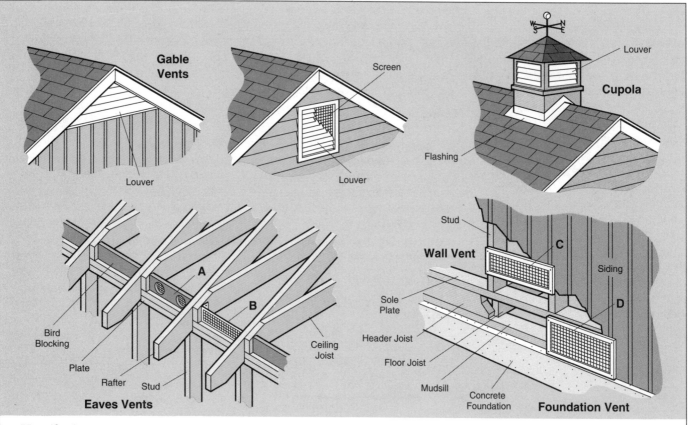

Ventilation. Gable vents are installed at each gable end to provide cross ventilation. Cupola allows air to escape at roof peak. Eaves vents can be simple 2-inch screened holes in bird blocking (A) of prefab sheet-metal vents installed between rafters (B). Wall vent (C) admits cool air at floor level; foundation vent (D) provides air circulation in enclosed space under shed floor.

Building Codes & Permits

Building codes generally deal with the structural integrity of the building (framing, wiring, plumbing, and so forth), while municipal or local ordinances dictate its size, location, and intended use. Some urban municipalities have additional regulations that govern the architectural style of the building, or even what colors you can paint it. If you're building the shed primarily for storage or as an unheated workspace, one set of codes and regulations will apply. However, if you start adding plumbing, wiring, heating, and interior walls—and still call it a storage shed—you'll probably be questioned and additional codes will come into play. And still another set of rules may apply if the shed is designed to house poultry or livestock.

Permits. In some localities, you may not need a building permit if the shed or barn is under a certain size, such as 120 square feet or less, and is not built on a permanent foundation. Specific rules vary from one community to another, but a permanent foundation is usually defined as a concrete slab or one that incorporates poured-concrete footings. In effect, the building department may make a distinction between "permanent" and "temporary" structures. If you add plumbing or wiring, you'll need separate permits for these. In all cases, check with building authorities to see if a permit is required.

Variances. If your plan does not conform with all local codes and ordinances, you can apply for a variance to have the nonconforming aspects waived by the local building authorities. However, you must present a good case for their doing so, and variance applications usually involve an additional fee—whether the variance is approved or not. Unless you have a compelling reason to do so, try not to involve variances in your plans.

Working Drawings. If the shed is very large or of a complex design, the building department may want to see a set of working drawings, including a floor plan and elevation views. These should show framing details, exact locations of doors and windows, roof type and pitch, and other significant architectural details. Even if the department doesn't require them, a set of working drawings will help you estimate materials and can serve as a framing guide.

Selecting a Site

If the shed is to be used for storing household items or as a workshop, you'll want it near the house, but not so close that it presents a fire hazard or blocks sunlight or views through adjacent house windows. On the other hand, if the new structure is to house poultry or livestock, you'll want it a good distance away from—and downwind of—the house. Codes usually dictate minimum distances between buildings. If the shed will house frequently used garden equipment, locate it convenient to garden areas. Also determine how the shed will affect present traffic patterns in your yard. Plan for convenient walkways or clear paths between the shed and the house, garage, and garden areas. Before building a large shed, decide if you want vehicle access for loading and unloading items to be stored in the shed. And determine what effect an access road will have on your landscaping. If your property is large enough, a circular drive would be ideal. While you're at it, decide how you want to orient the shed itself—that is, which direction the door should face to provide the most convenient access.

Lot contours and soil conditions may also influence where you locate the shed. Avoid placing it in a low, poorly drained area or on a steep slope. Siting the shed on level, well-drained soil will minimize grading and foundation requirements.

Conditions such as sun, shade, and wind are usually not too important when siting a storage shed. But if the shed will house animals or serve as a workshop, you'll want to situate it to provide maximum protection from cold winter winds, while taking advantage of summer breezes for good ventilation. Placing the shed among deciduous trees will keep it shaded in summer and allow sun to pass through during the winter months. You can orient the shed with the long dimension facing south to make the most of solar gain during cold-weather months. Try to place the entry door and windows away from prevailing winter winds. At the same time, keep in mind the best position of windows and vents to catch summer's cooling breezes.

If you want to wire the shed for lights or electrical outlets, you'll need to run an overhead wire or underground cable from the service entrance (or a convenient junction box) at your house. Site the shed to provide a direct, clear path for a utility line through the yard. Also, do not build the shed directly over existing underground pipes or utility lines.

If you have a small yard, potential shed sites (and sizes) will be limited. You'll want to consider the visual impact on both your own house and yard and those of your neighbors. It's a good idea to let your neighbors know of your plans, to avoid disputes once the shed is built. Also determine how shade cast by the shed throughout the year will affect surrounding plantings, decks, patios, and other landscape features.

After you've decided the type of shed you want and its size, determine where it will go on the property. Bear in mind that in most communities, sheds and other permanent buildings must be set back a certain distance from property lines and other buildings (see Building Codes and Permits, page 9), so check with your local building department before choosing the final location for your shed.

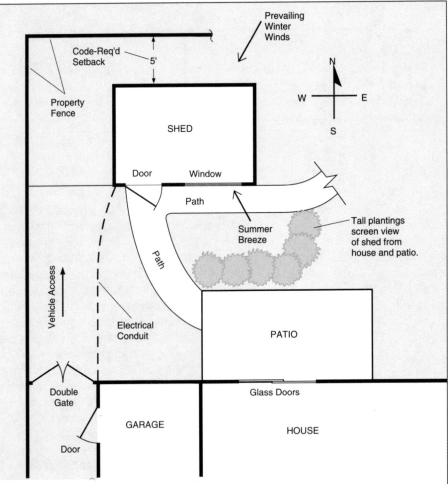

Selecting a Site. Among the factors to consider in locating a shed are vehicle and personal access, prevailing winds, wiring needs, lines of sight, and setbacks required by building codes.

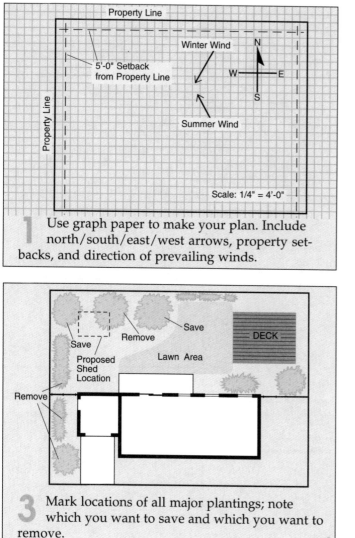

1 Use graph paper to make your plan. Include north/south/east/west arrows, property setbacks, and direction of prevailing winds.

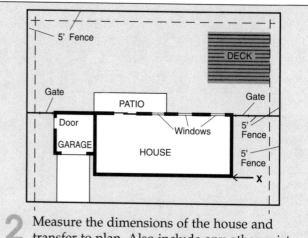

2 Measure the dimensions of the house and transfer to plan. Also include any other existing structures.

3 Mark locations of all major plantings; note which you want to save and which you want to remove.

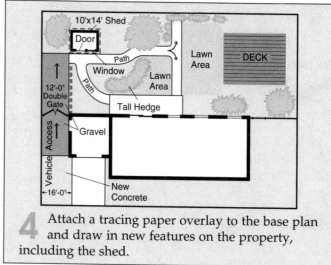

4 Attach a tracing paper overlay to the base plan and draw in new features on the property, including the shed.

Making a Site Plan

1 Marking Property Lines. Use the grid paper on the next page to make your plan. A scale of ¼ inch = 4 feet should enable you to put the entire plan on the grid. If not, use a larger sheet. Start by marking the property lines, as shown. Indicate north, south, east, and west, and mark directions of prevailing summer and winter winds, if these are a factor. Check with the building department to find out how far the building must be set back from the lot lines; mark these setback limits as dotted lines on your plan.

2 Locating Existing Structures. Starting from a front corner of the house (marked X on the drawing), measure the dimensions of the house and transfer them to the plan. Include the locations of exterior doors and windows on the wall or walls facing the shed. Measure and mark the locations of other buildings and permanent structures, including patios, decks, fences, and concrete walks. Also show any underground or overhead fixtures, such as utility lines and septic systems.

3 Locating Plantings. Mark the locations of trees, shrubs, and other major plantings and specify which ones are to be kept and which will need to be removed or relocated.

On sloping sites, the building department may require spot elevations or grade contours to be indicated on the plan. This plan will serve as your base map for siting the shed.

4 Locating the Shed on Overlays. Attach an overlay of tracing paper to the base map. Draw in the exact size and location of the proposed shed, including the locations of doors and windows, roof overhang, new utility lines, new plantings, and any walks or driveways leading to the shed. Use as many overlay sheets as needed to come up with a suitable plan. Draw the final overlay neatly and submit it with your base map when you apply for a building permit.

BEFORE YOU BUILD

As with any building, sheds are built from the ground up. Before you start building, you'll need to identify the various structural components that make up the four major elements of a shed: the foundation, floor, walls, and roof. This chapter opens with a discussion of the materials required to build these. Then it details the basic tools and hardware you'll need.

Materials

Once your plans are approved, you can start estimating and ordering materials. Practically all of the materials you'll need are readily available at lumberyards. However, you may have to special-order some items, such as doors, windows, or siding. If so, place your order several weeks in advance of the proposed building date so these items will be on hand when you need them. Following is a general discussion of the materials you'll need. Specific material lists are provided for each of the four shed designs in this book (pages 49, 50, 54, and 57).

Foundation Materials

The options for shed foundations depend on soil and climatic conditions, the size and intended use of the shed, and local building codes. Ideally, the concrete footings for the foundation will extend down to undisturbed soil or rock. In cold climates, the footings must also extend below the frost line, which varies in different parts of the country, and can be as deep as 48 inches in the coldest part of the country. Consult your local building department for accepted practices in your area.

Other than the wood foundation described below, all foundations will require wet concrete; to estimate amounts, see Mixing and Pouring Concrete (page 22).

Wood Foundations. Small, lightweight utility or garden sheds may not require a concrete foundation. You can build them directly on pressure-treated beams or railroad ties laid on firm, level, well-drained soil or on 3 to 4 inches of compacted gravel or crushed rock. Although simple and inexpensive, this on-ground foundation may be a poor choice for sites with shifting or boggy soil, or soil that is subject to severe winter frost heaves. Use only pressure-treated beams or timbers that are rated for on-ground or below-ground

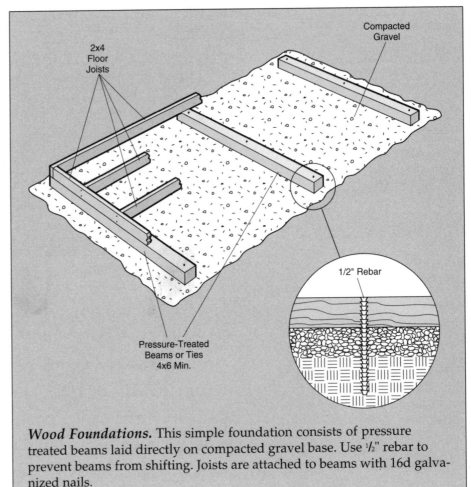

Wood Foundations. This simple foundation consists of pressure treated beams laid directly on compacted gravel base. Use ½" rebar to prevent beams from shifting. Joists are attached to beams with 16d galvanized nails.

contact. To prevent the beams from shifting, secure them with ½-inch reinforcing bars (also called rebar) inserted through holes drilled in the beams and driven 3 to 4 feet into the ground. Attach the floor joists directly to the leveled beams, as shown. Leave each side or end of the foundation open to promote drainage and air circulation beneath the floor.

Concrete Foundations. You have four choices here: precast piers, poured-concrete piers, a perimeter foundation, and a concrete slab. Pier foundations (either precast or poured) require the least excavation, formwork, and concrete. If the ground is stable, you can set precast piers directly on firm, compacted soil. For a sturdier foundation, they can be set in concrete footings. Posts, beams, or joists are attached to wood nailing blocks on the pier.

Similar to precast piers, poured-concrete piers are made by pouring concrete into a wooden form, which you make yourself, or a cardboard-tube form (available at building suppliers) set into the ground. You can set the cardboard tubes to any depth below ground and any height above by cutting them to the desired length. Tubes provide the best foundation if you're building on a sloping or uneven site because the piers can easily be poured to various heights to create a level floor without having to level the ground beneath.

Perimeter foundations are more permanent and provide more support than piers; they're suitable for larger barns and sheds. Such foundations can be poured so the finish floor height is as low as 6 inches above ground, but you must provide ventilation beneath the floor to prevent rot.

Nominal Size	Actual Size	Nominal Size	Actual Size
1×2	$3/4 \times 1^1/_2$	2×4	$1^1/_2 \times 3^1/_2$
1×3	$3/4 \times 2^1/_2$	2×6	$1^1/_2 \times 5^1/_2$
1×4	$3/4 \times 3^1/_2$	2×8	$1^1/_2 \times 7^1/_4$
1×6	$3/4 \times 5^1/_2$	2×10	$1^1/_2 \times 9^1/_4$
1×8	$3/4 \times 7^1/_4$	2×12	$1^1/_2 \times 11^1/_4$
1×10	$3/4 \times 9^1/_4$		
1×12	$3/4 \times 11^1/_4$	4×4	$3^1/_2 \times 3^1/_2$
		6×6	$5^1/_2 \times 5^1/_2$
		8×8	$7^1/_2 \times 7^1/_2$

Approximate number of nails per pound of various sizes

Penny Size	Length	Common	Finishing
2d	1"	870	1,350
3d	$1^1/_4$"	543	850
4d	$1^1/_2$"	290	600
5d	$1^5/_8$"	254	300
6d	2"	236	200
7d	$2^1/_8$"	223	125
8d	$2^1/_2$"	135	
10d	3"	92	
12d	$3^1/_4$"	61	
16d	$3^1/_2$"	47	
20d	4"	29	
30d	$4^1/_2$"	22	
40d	5"	17	
50d	$5^1/_2$"	13	
60d	6"	10	

Concrete slabs make the sturdiest foundations, provided they're thick enough. Although they often require more concrete than a perimeter foundation, they're easier to install because less formwork is required. Because the slab also acts as the floor, no floor framing is required. This enables you to install the floor an inch or two above ground level—a logical choice for storing heavy wheeled equipment. For specific building details on concrete foundations, see pages 20–30.

Framing Lumber

In most parts of the country, fir, hemlock, or southern yellow pine is used for all framing members above floor level (plates, studs, rafters, ceiling joists, and the like). It's best to use kiln-dried lumber because it's readily available and easy to work with. Kiln-dried lumber is sawed and planed to exact dimensions, which are somewhat smaller than their nominal size (for example, a 2x4 actually measures 1½ inches by 3½ inches—see the chart above). Although less expensive, rough-sawn "green" or "garden grade" lumber is usually not recommended for framing buildings because it is wet, heavy, rough-textured, and not always milled to exact dimensions. As the boards dry out, they shrink, split, and warp. However, green lumber is sometimes used for board-and-batten siding because of its rustic appearance.

Framing lumber is graded according to the number of knots, checks, splits, and other defects found in the board. Avoid lumber with large knots, checks, splits, or missing wood (called wane) because these will weaken the structure. And keep in mind that badly warped, twisted, or bowed boards will make the framing job considerably more difficult.

Pressure-Treated Lumber. Codes may require you to use pressure-treated lumber for foundation and subfloor members (posts, beams, mudsills, and floor joists). If the members come in direct contact with the ground or a concrete footing, they should be rated for ground-contact use; treated lumber rated for above-ground use may be used for suspended members such as beams and floor joists. In some localities, a naturally decay-resistant species such as redwood or red cedar may also be used for foundation members. However, these species are usually more expensive than pressure-treated lumber, and only the darker heartwood effectively resists decay. If you do go with one of these woods, use "construction heart" grade.

Flooring Materials

A concrete slab makes the best floor for sheds because it supports extremely heavy loads and is relatively easy to keep clean. Exterior plywood is the best material for wood-frame shed floors, especially if one side of the shed will be left open to the weather. In most cases, 3/4-inch plywood is sufficient; for a sturdier floor, use 1¼-inch tongue-and-groove plywood or two layers of thinner plywood (such as 3/4-inch covered with 1/2-inch). If two layers are used, place the top sheets at right angles to the bottom ones, staggering the joints.

Other options include tongue-and-groove 2-by wood planks nailed directly to floor joists, or 1-by boards over a plywood subfloor. Particleboard should not be used as a finish floor material.

Sheathing and Siding

The best material for roof sheathing is 1/2-inch exterior CDX plywood. The "X" in CDX stands for exterior grade. It means the plywood is intended for outdoor sheathing that will be covered with roofing or siding. It is not intended to be left permanently exposed to the weather. A less expensive sheathing alternative is waferboard. Also called chipboard, waferboard is made of resin-impregnated wood chips boned under high pressure to form panels.

The most econimical way to make durable shed walls is to cover them with plywood siding. These plywood sheets are designed to be permanently exposed, and because they are plywood they eliminate the structural need for separate sheathing. Plywood siding comes in several surface patterns. The most familiar plywood siding is called Textured 1-11, or T-1-11 for short. It has a rough sawn texture with narrow, evenly-spaced grooves to simulate vertical board siding.

Wood-board sidings come in a wide variety of board styles and can be applied vertically or horizontally. On long walls, you may need to install diagonal bracing if the boards are nailed directly to the studs. A sampling of board styles is shown on page 62.

Other siding options include hardboard, vinyl, aluminum, and steel. Hardboard siding comes in 4×8 panels, as well as several different "board" styles with smooth or wood-grained textures. It is installed much like conventional wood-board siding or plywood siding. Vinyl, steel, and aluminum sidings also simulate hori-

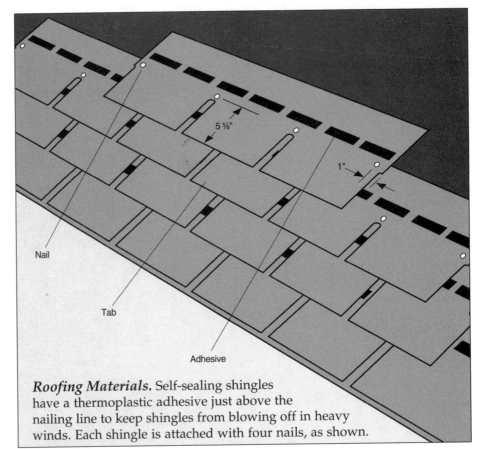

Roofing Materials. Self-sealing shingles have a thermoplastic adhesive just above the nailing line to keep shingles from blowing off in heavy winds. Each shingle is attached with four nails, as shown.

zontal or vertical board patterns. Installation requirements for vinyl siding are discussed on pages 67–68.

Roofing Materials

The most popular roofing materials for sheds are asphalt shingles and asphalt roll roofing. Traditional cedar shakes and shingles are another option, but many communities prohibit these because they present a fire hazard. If you do decide to install cedar shakes or shingles, make sure they are treated with a fire retardant and otherwise conform to local building codes and ordinances.

Other roofing materials include 15-pound building felt (installed between the shingles and the roof sheathing) and metal flashings and drip edges, both of which are installed to ensure a watertight roof.

Trim and Fascia

If you're installing vinyl, aluminum, or steel siding, special metal or vinyl trims and fascias are usually included in the package. And with wood-board or plywood siding, you can choose from a wide variety of wood trim and fascia profiles. The widest selection is usually in fir or pine, although redwood or cedar fascia will last much longer. These species are usually more expensive, and molding profiles are limited. Also bear in mind that redwood and cedar are "bleeding" species; that is, the tannins in the wood will bleed through light-colored paint, discoloring it. A shellac-based wood primer will minimize this effect. If you choose pine or fir fascia and trim, treat the pieces with a wood preservative and/or water repellent (such as Thompson's Water Seal) to help resist decay. Typical applications for trim and fascias are shown on pages 43, 64, and 76.

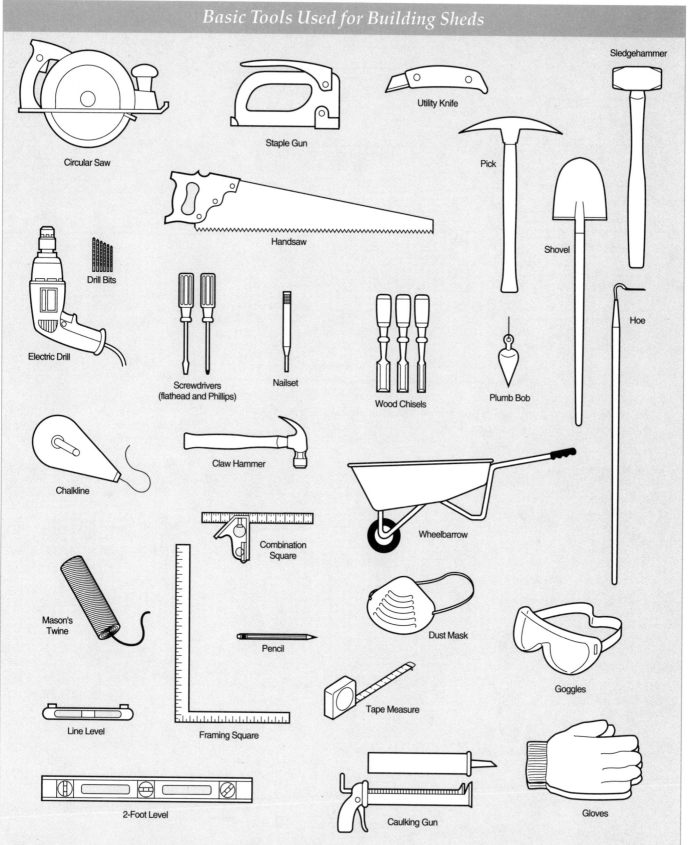

Circular Saw

Staple Gun

Utility Knife

Sledgehammer

Pick

Shovel

Handsaw

Drill Bits

Electric Drill

Screwdrivers
(flathead and Phillips)

Nailset

Wood Chisels

Plumb Bob

Hoe

Chalkline

Claw Hammer

Wheelbarrow

Combination
Square

Mason's
Twine

Pencil

Dust Mask

Goggles

Line Level

Framing Square

Tape Measure

2-Foot Level

Caulking Gun

Gloves

The basic tools and equipment shown above are essential for preparing the site, mixing and pouring concrete, and building the shed itself. Other specialized tools and materials are listed as needed for various phases of construction described in this book. A range of nail sizes and counts is given at the top of page 15.

Fasteners

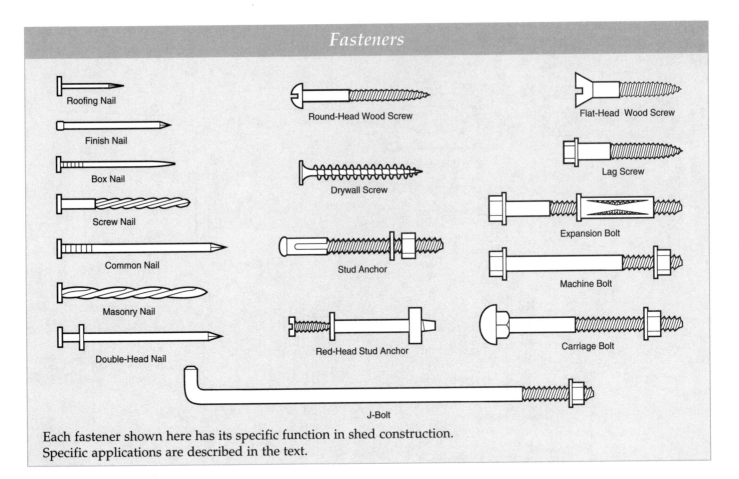

Each fastener shown here has its specific function in shed construction. Specific applications are described in the text.

Connectors

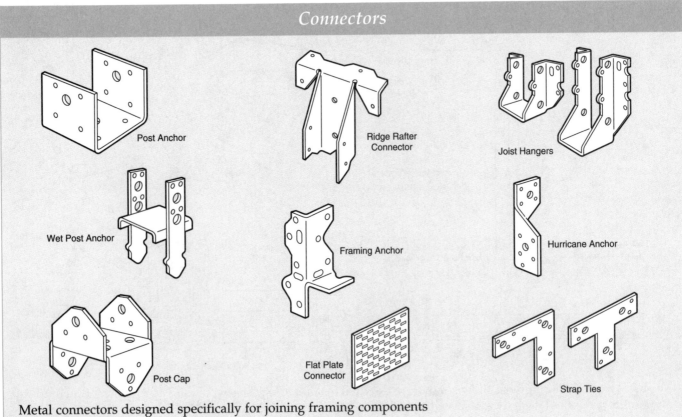

Metal connectors designed specifically for joining framing components provide a much stronger connection than nails or screws alone.

FOUNDATIONS

This chapter describes how to lay out and install several types of foundations for sheds. The type you choose depends largely on the size of the shed and soil conditions. Consult your building department for specific requirements. Foundation options are described on pages 14–15.

1. Before you order building materials, clear the construction area. Remove all shrubs, rocks, grass, weeds, tree roots, and other debris on the shed site. Be sure to remove all wood scraps because they may attract termites.

Clear a second area near the shed site for storing lumber, plywood, siding, sacks of concrete, and other building materials. Ideally, these materials should be kept under cover. If this isn't possible, neatly place lumber and plywood in stacks above the ground, then cover the stacks with a tarp or plastic sheeting.

Determine if you need to provide truck or trailer access to the site for delivery of wet concrete or large amounts of lumber and other materials. If so, you may have to remove a section of fence or relocate shrubs or other plantings to provide a clear path for the truck.

2. Make sure the ground slopes away from the shed site at least 10 feet in all directions. If necessary, build up the soil in the center of the site and slope it away from the high point to provide drainage. Fill in any low spots within the perimeter of the site. A slope of 1/8 inch per foot is enough to prevent water accumulation.

3. If the site cannot be sloped or graded to provide sufficient drainage, you'll need to install an underground drainage system. This usually consists of a perforated drainpipe buried in a gravel-filled trench around the perimeter of the shed foundation, and leading to a dry well located at a lower part of the property. Dig the trench 2 to 3 feet deep and fill the bottom with about 4 inches of gravel. Lay perforated drainpipe in the trench, holes facing down. Backfill the trench with gravel to within 6 inches of the top. Cover the gravel with porous mesh fabric designed for this purpose, then fill the remainder of the trench with topsoil (the fabric prevents the topsoil from filtering into the gravel).

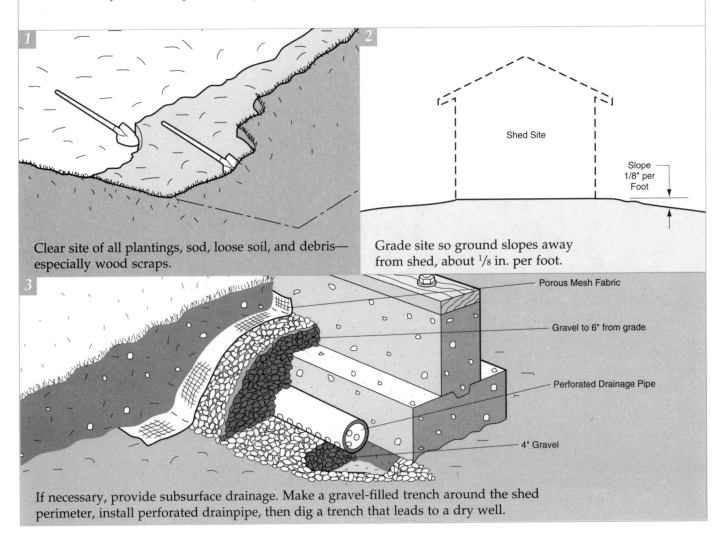

1 Clear site of all plantings, sod, loose soil, and debris—especially wood scraps.

2 Grade site so ground slopes away from shed, about 1/8 in. per foot.

Shed Site

Slope 1/8" per Foot

3 If necessary, provide subsurface drainage. Make a gravel-filled trench around the shed perimeter, install perforated drainpipe, then dig a trench that leads to a dry well.

Porous Mesh Fabric

Gravel to 6" from grade

Perforated Drainage Pipe

4" Gravel

Laying Out the Foundation

1 Staking Out the Shed. No matter which type of foundation you've chosen, start by outlining the shed's "footprint" on the site with string and batter boards. Bear in mind that even if the shed is some distance from the house, you should build it parallel or at right angles to the house. Choose one corner of the shed near the house, a wall face, or other structure, and mark it by driving a stake into the ground.

2 Setting Up Batter Boards. Set up two batter boards, as shown here, about 1 foot outside the first stake. Drive a nail into the board that is at right angles to the structure to which you are orienting the shed, and from that nail run a line parallel to the structure across the stake. Measure the desired dimension of the shed along that line and drive another stake. Set up batter boards in the same way at that location.

3 Measuring by Triangulation. Measure along the line 3 feet from the first stake A, and mark the string at this point. From stake A, run a second line perpendicular to the first. Measure out 4 feet to locate point C. If this second line is exactly at a right angle to the first, the diagonal between the 4-foot point C and the 3-foot point B will be exactly 5 feet, and you have a right triangle. If it is not 5 feet, move point C left or right until the diagonal measures 5 feet, and stake that point.

4 Outlining the Shed. Stretch a line from stake A straight across C and fasten it to a temporary stake outside the intended shed area. Measure along this line from A and mark the shed dimension in that direction. Drive a stake there and set up batter boards. Then use the 3-4-5 triangulation method to extend another line at right angles to the A-C line (it will run parallel to line A-B). Measure to the next corner and stake it. Continue until all corners of the shed area are connected by right-angle lines.

Check the accuracy of the layout by measuring the diagonals between opposite corners. If they are equal, all corners are right angles.

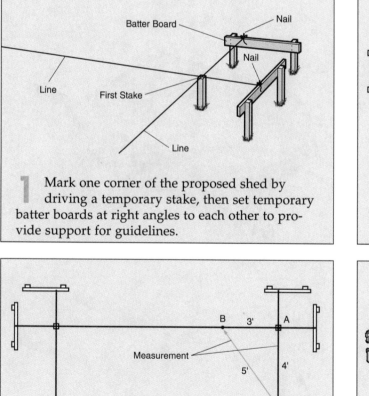

1 Mark one corner of the proposed shed by driving a temporary stake, then set temporary batter boards at right angles to each other to provide support for guidelines.

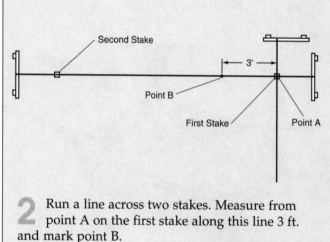

2 Run a line across two stakes. Measure from point A on the first stake along this line 3 ft. and mark point B.

3 Run a second line perpendicular to the first across point A. Mark point C 4 ft. from point A. Move line AC so that the distance BC is exactly 5 ft. Angle BAC is now 90 degrees.

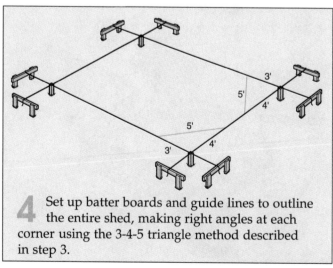

4 Set up batter boards and guide lines to outline the entire shed, making right angles at each corner using the 3-4-5 triangle method described in step 3.

Should you mix your own concrete or have it delivered by truck, ready to pour? That depends on how much concrete you need and whether you would rather spend time and effort on mixing or spend money on premixed concrete.

If you only need to make a few footings for piers, buy sacks of dry mix. One 90-pound sack will make $2/3$ cubic foot of concrete, which equals one 12×12×8-inch footing, the standard size. (A 12×12×6-inch footing equals $1/2$ cubic foot, and a 12×12×12-inch footing equals 1 cubic foot.)

1. You can mix up 3 or 4 cubic feet of concrete in a wheelbarrow. Dump in the required amount of dry mix and stir it thoroughly with a shovel or hoe. You will need about 4 gallons of water for 3 cubic feet and 5 gallons for 4 cubic feet.

2. Scoop out a hollow in the middle of the dry mix and pour in about half of the water.

3. Mix everything thoroughly. Add the remaining water a little at a time and mix constantly. Do not let any dry material accumulate.

4. Watch the consistency of the concrete carefully. Wet concrete should be stiff, mounding easily into a stable cone; it should not slosh around or be dry and crumbly. When a batch is ready, pour the footings immediately. If you are using precast piers on top of fresh concrete, put them in place immediately and align them. Insert metal connectors into the concrete at once and make sure they are level and aligned.

For perimeter footings or concrete slabs, order premixed concrete. Before doing so, carefully estimate the amount you will need. A 10×12-foot slab 4 inches thick requires about $1^1/3$ cubic yards. Premixed concrete is usually sold by the cubic yard, which is 27 cubic feet. Find out what quantity your supplier will deliver and at what price. Be ready to pour the foundation when the truck pulls up; have a wheelbarrow handy.

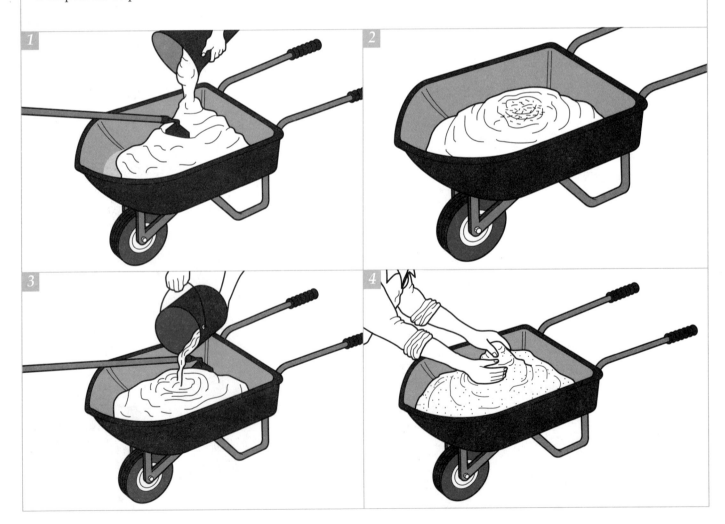

Pier Foundations

Pier foundations are the simplest type you can use, and take the least concrete. Several variations exist; a few of the more common types are shown on the following pages. These include precast pier blocks, poured-concrete pier blocks (which require a simple wooden form), and cardboard-tube forms. The type you choose depends on the nature of the soil. Precast pier blocks usually come with integral wooden nailing blocks to which you attach posts or beams. With some precast piers you simply toenail beams or posts to the wooden block. Other pier blocks come with metal post anchors attached to the wood block.

With poured-concrete piers, you usually set a post anchor or similar metal connector into the wet concrete, then attach the post or beam to the connector. The number of piers needed, and the spacing between them depend on the type of floor framing you'll be installing (see page 32).

1 Locating the Corner Footing Holes. Using the string and batter boards as a guide, locate footing holes at each of the four corners. Bear in mind that the intersections of the strings represent the outside corners of the shed floor; dig the footing holes and position the piers so that the outside corners of the beams or posts, when attached to the piers, will align with the intersecting strings. Use a plumb line to find this spot on the ground beneath the intersecting strings. Then drive a stake into the ground inside this spot to mark the post center, until it is time to dig the hole.

2 Locating Intermediate Footing Holes. Next, measure along each string to locate the rest of the footing holes around the perimeter between the corner holes; drop a plumb line at each location and mark the spot with a stake. Footings inside the perimeter can be located by cen-

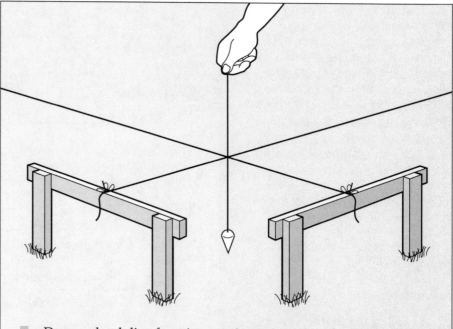

1 Drop a plumb line from intersecting strings at each corner of the shed, then mark the ground with a stake to locate the footing hole.

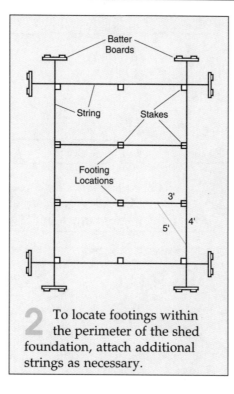

2 To locate footings within the perimeter of the shed foundation, attach additional strings as necessary.

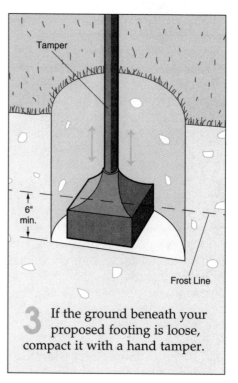

3 If the ground beneath your proposed footing is loose, compact it with a hand tamper.

tering strings between perimeter footings and squaring them, using the 3-4-5 triangulation method described on page 21.

3 Digging Footing Holes. Use a shovel or post-hole digger to dig holes at the staked positions. For adequate support, the footing hole must extend at least 6 inches below the frost line. To avoid using excess concrete, dig narrow, straight-walled holes. If you're digging the holes in loose soil, compact the bottom of the footing hole with a hand tamper as shown.

4 Installing Piers. If using precast pier blocks, pour wet concrete into the holes within 3 to 6 inches of ground level. While the concrete is still plastic but stiff enough to support the pier without sinking, embed the pier 1 to 2 inches in the footing, aligning the outside edges of the blocks to the batter-board strings. The top of the pier block should be at least 3 inches above ground level. Place a level diagonally across the top of the pier in both directions to level it.

If using tube forms, set these into the hole and brace them, as shown at right. Other options are shown on the facing page.

5 Leveling the Piers. If the beams or floor joists will be attached directly to the piers, you'll need to level them all to the same height. You can do this by placing a long, straight 2×4 across the tops of the piers along one side of the perimeter, and a 2-foot level atop the board (for larger foundations, use a string and line level). Adjust the pier or tube heights until the board is level and in contact with all the piers in the row; for piers, add more wet concrete, if needed, to raise them. Repeat for the other three sides, and any intermediate piers within the perimeter. After the concrete sets, correct any minor out-of-level conditions by driving cedar shims between the pier tops and the joists or beams when you attach them. If posts will be attached to the piers to support beams or joists, the pier height needn't be adjusted.

6 Using Unfooted Pier Blocks. For a small shed built low to the ground, pier blocks placed directly on the ground, without any poured footing, can provide sufficient support. Posts are attached to the pier blocks by way of metal connectors, as shown, or wood nailing blocks atop the piers.

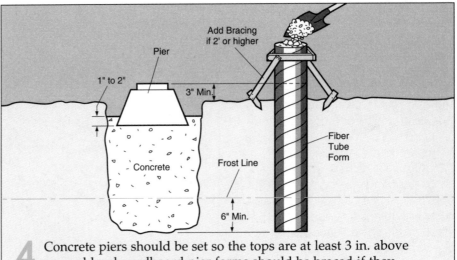

4 Concrete piers should be set so the tops are at least 3 in. above ground level; cardboard pier forms should be braced if they extend 2 ft. or higher above the ground.

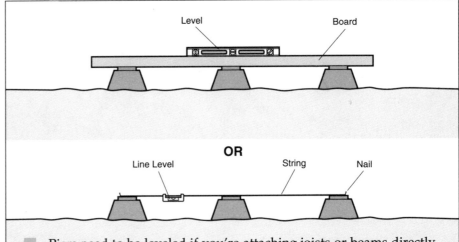

5 Piers need to be leveled if you're attaching joists or beams directly to them. Use a level and straight board for small foundations, line level and string for large foundations.

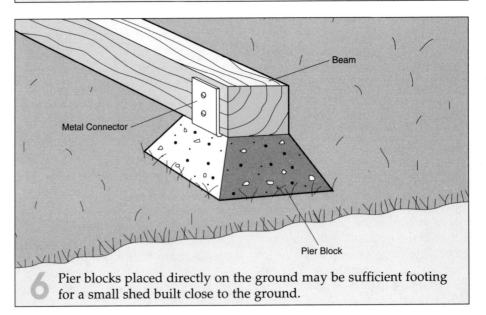

6 Pier blocks placed directly on the ground may be sufficient footing for a small shed built close to the ground.

Form

Poured Concrete

In soft ground, dig a larger hole and set a wood form over it so that 5 or 6 inches of concrete sits above ground level. A metal connector embedded in the concrete footing is bolted to the bottom of the post.

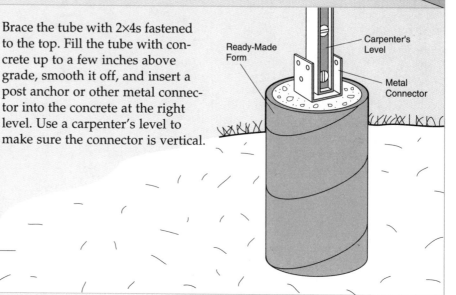

Connector

A ready-made cardboard pier form is especially useful in sandy or gravel-like soils. It consists of a waxed cardboard tube that keeps the surrounding soil from falling into the space where the concrete will be poured. Tubes are available in a range of sizes.

Make the diameter of the posthole a little bigger than the diameter of the ready-made tube. Cut off the tube a little above the level you want the concrete to be. Place it in the post hole. Compact soil around the tube to make sure that it is stable and will not shift.

Brace the tube with 2×4s fastened to the top. Fill the tube with concrete up to a few inches above grade, smooth it off, and insert a post anchor or other metal connector into the concrete at the right level. Use a carpenter's level to make sure the connector is vertical.

Ready-Made Form

Carpenter's Level

Metal Connector

In northern climates where severe freezing occurs, the cement in the ready-made tube may crack unless it is reinforced with a steel rod. Insert a No. 5 size steel reinforcing rod in the tube, just short of the desired height. In areas that experience severe freezing, codes may specify that footings be placed below frost level to avoid heaving that could damage the shed. After all the footings have been poured and the connectors put in place, wait three days and then remove the bracing, forms, and cardboard from the concrete.

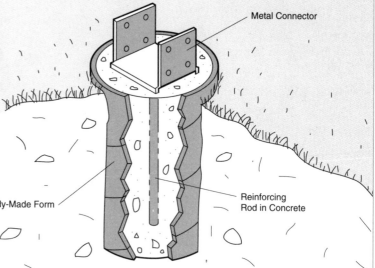

Metal Connector

Ready-Made Form

Reinforcing Rod in Concrete

Poured-Concrete Perimeter Foundation

There are two types of poured-concrete perimeter foundations. One is a simple footing, 8 to 16 inches wide, which you make in a single pour. The footing extends several inches above ground level; the depth depends on soil conditions and the weight of the building the foundation must support. This type of footing is suitable for small sheds in mild climates where there is little or no frost heave. Check with your local building department to see if this alternative meets local codes and is suitable for your area.

In climates subject to frost heave, you'll need to pour a concrete foundation with a separate footing, as shown at right. Two sets of forms are required—one for the footing and another for the foundation wall. The trench must be wide enough to accommodate the braced forms as well as the footing and foundation itself; two separate pours are required. The footing must be poured below the frost line, and is keyed into the wall as shown. Both the footing and foundation wall are strengthened with reinforcing bars. After the wall is poured, insert anchor bolts into the wet concrete with which to attach the mudsill.

1 Digging the Footing Trench. Using your batter boards and strings as guides, dig the footing trench to the desired width and depth. A trench for a 12-inch-thick footing, for example, should be about 8½ inches deep. This enables you to build forms so that the top of the concrete footing will be about 3 inches above ground level (Step 2). If the soil is loose at the bottom of the trench, compact it with a tamper.

To keep the trench depth at a consistent level, drop a plumb line at frequent intervals along the batter-board strings around the shed perimeter. Remember that the original

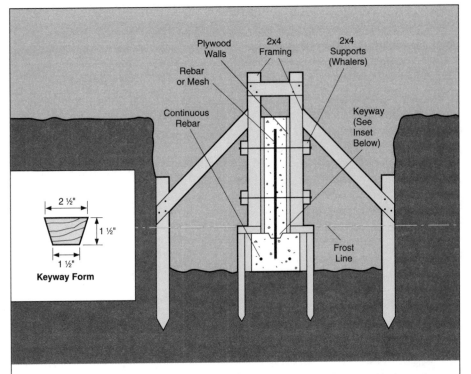

Poured Concrete Perimeter Foundation. A poured concrete foundation with separate footing is used in cold climates subject to frost heave.

Note: Because of the extensive excavation, formwork, and large amounts of concrete required, this type of foundation is best left to an experienced contractor.

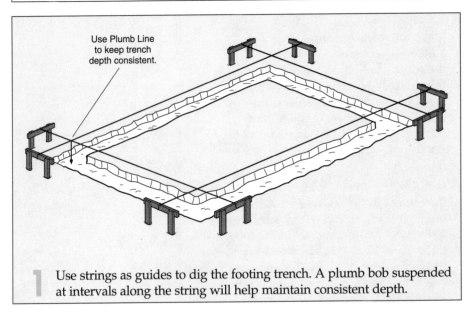

1 Use strings as guides to dig the footing trench. A plumb bob suspended at intervals along the string will help maintain consistent depth.

string locations represent the outside walls of the shed; you must position the trench and the foundation forms (Step 2) so that the outside edges of the mudsills (Step 4) align with the strings. The mudsills themselves will be the foundation members to which you attach the wall framing.

2 Building the Forms. Construct the forms as shown in the drawing. The footing thickness should equal the width of the boards plus ½ inch. An 12-inch-thick footing, for example, uses 1×12s (or two 1×6s) suspended ½ inch above the bottom of the trench. It's okay if some concrete spills out beneath the forms, as this will help provide a more solid base for the footing. Nail the boards to 1×2 or 2×4 stakes spaced 18 to 24 inches apart. Then attach 1×2 braces across the top of the forms every 2 feet to keep them from spreading when you pour the concrete into them. The top of the forms should be from 2 to 3 inches above ground level. Check the inside and outside corners of the forms to make sure that they meet at right angles; use the 3-4-5 triangulation method described on page 21. Before you pour the concrete, brush the insides of the forms with a light coat of motor oil; this will make them easier to remove after the concrete hardens.

3 **Pouring the Concrete.** Lay ½-inch reinforcing bars (rebar) in the trench. Use stones or pieces of broken concrete to suspend the rebar several inches from the bottom of the trench. With a helper, pour or shovel wet concrete into the forms, flush to the top. As you pour, use a shovel or hoe to work out any air pockets in the concrete. Use a wood float, flat trowel, or short length of 2×4 to screed and smooth the top surface of the footing.

4 **Attaching the Mudsill.** While the concrete is still wet, insert anchor bolts, spaced 2 feet apart, into the footing, as shown. After the concrete hardens (in one to two hours), attach the mudsill to the anchor bolts and level it. Mudsills are typically 2×4 or 2×6 pressure-treated lumber. Allow the concrete to cure fully (seven to ten days) before removing the forms. Then backfill the trench with a layer of gravel, followed by a layer of topsoil. Make sure the ground slopes away from the footing on all sides. If subsurface drainage is needed (page 20), install it before you backfill the trench.

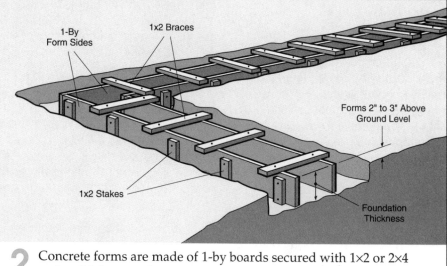

2 Concrete forms are made of 1-by boards secured with 1×2 or 2×4 stakes. Make sure the corners meet at 90-degree angles.

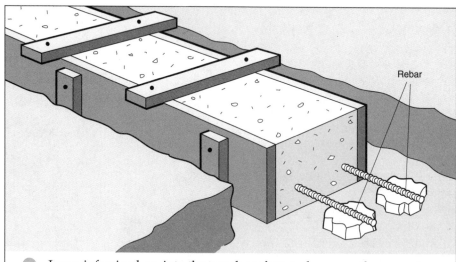

3 Lay reinforcing bars into the trench as shown, then pour the concrete flush with the top of the forms. Smooth with a float or flat trowel.

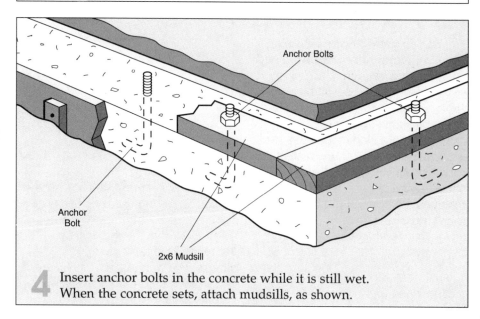

4 Insert anchor bolts in the concrete while it is still wet. When the concrete sets, attach mudsills, as shown.

Concrete-Slab Foundation

Requirements for a concrete-slab foundation vary, depending on climate, soil conditions, and the weight of the structure it must support. For small sheds, the slab is typically 3 to 4 inches thick, laid over a subbase of 4 inches of gravel or crushed rock. A plastic vapor barrier sandwiched between the gravel and concrete keeps subsurface moisture from seeping up through the slab.

The slab perimeter has a thickened footing to support the shed walls. In most cases, the footing is 6 to 12 inches thick; the slab and footing can be made in one pour and only one set of forms is required.

If the perimeter footing needs to be much deeper, you'll have to pour it separately, using the methods described on page 26. The slab is then poured within the perimeter foundation, separated by an isolation joint, as shown at lower right. The isolation joint is a preformed material, about 1/2 inch thick, that comes in various widths.

In slab construction, the weight of the wet concrete will apply more outward pressure on the forms than it would in a simple perimeter foundation, so 2-by form boards and stakes should be used.

The slab is reinforced with 6×6-inch No. 10 wire mesh or a grid of 1/2-inch rebar. Rebar is also placed in the footings, as for a perimeter foundation.

If frost heave is a problem, you may need to provide additional reinforcement to keep the slab from cracking. In areas with extreme frost heave, concrete slabs usually aren't recommended; consult a masonry contractor for the accepted practices in your area.

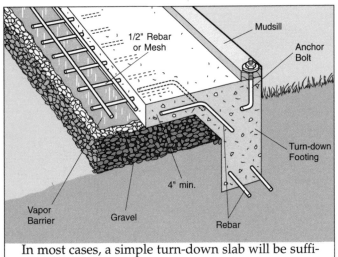

In most cases, a simple turn-down slab will be sufficient to support the shed. Check local codes for slab/footing thickness.

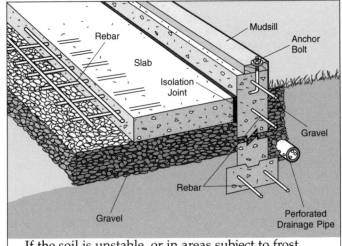

If the soil is unstable, or in areas subject to frost heave, a separate foundation wall and footing may be required.

Building the Forms

1 Excavating the Slab Area and Footing Trench. Using your strings and batter boards as a guide, excavate the slab area and the footing trench to the desired depth. For example, if the slab is 4 inches thick, and you're backfilling underneath it with 4 inches of gravel, you would excavate the slab area to a depth of 6 inches. This would put the finished slab surface 2 inches above ground level. The depth of the footing trench depends on climatic and soil conditions in your area, and the size of the shed; follow the guidelines already discussed. If the soil in the bottom of

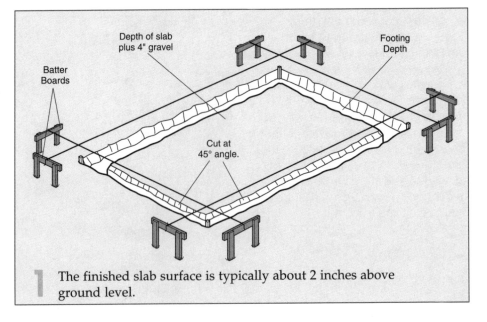

1 The finished slab surface is typically about 2 inches above ground level.

the excavation is loose or spongy, compact it with a hand tamper, or a power tamper rented from a tool rental company.

2 **Locating the Forms.** Set up your batter board strings to represent the outside face of the slab or footing (which also represents the inside face of the form boards). At each corner, drop a plumb line from the intersecting strings to the bottom of the trench, then drive a 2×4 stake at this point. Using the plumb bob again, drive a nail into the top of the stake where the plumb bob touches it. Attach strings between the stakes. Using the strings as guides, drive the 2×4 form stakes around the trench perimeter, spaced on 2-foot centers. The inside faces of the stakes should be away from the strings a distance equal to the thickness of the form boards. To accurately place the stakes, cut a spacer from the form material, as shown.

3 **Attaching the Form Boards.** Attach the form boards to the stakes with double-headed nails. Make sure the stakes are on the outside of the boards and flush with or below them. As you attach the boards, level and adjust them for height. Make sure each corner forms a 90-degree angle, using the 3-4-5 triangulation method described on page 21. After the boards are attached, double-check your work by measuring opposite diagonals, from corner to corner. If both diagonals are the same length, the forms are square.

4 **Bracing the Forms.** Use 2×4 stakes to brace the corners of the forms. If you must join two shorter boards together to make one long one, brace the joint as shown.

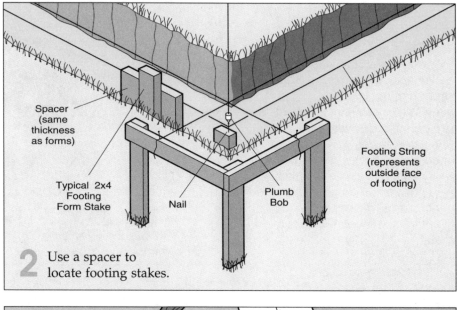

Spacer (same thickness as forms)

Typical 2x4 Footing Form Stake

Nail

Plumb Bob

Footing String (represents outside face of footing)

2 Use a spacer to locate footing stakes.

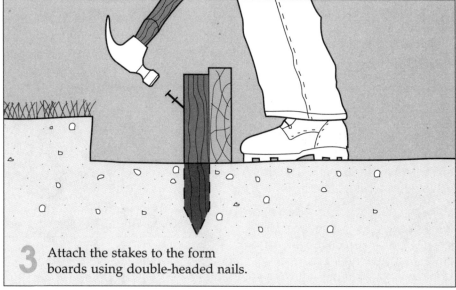

3 Attach the stakes to the form boards using double-headed nails.

4 Brace the form at each corner and any weak spots that you may find.

Pouring the Concrete

1 Preparing to Pour. Backfill the excavation with 4 inches of gravel, then lay down the plastic vapor barrier, if you're using one. Place wire mesh reinforcement or reinforcing rods over the slab area. Use small stones or pieces of brick or concrete to raise the reinforcement about 2 inches above the plastic. Also position rebar in the thickened perimeter footing, as shown on page 28. If the soil is dry, dampen it slightly a day or two before the pour. Mist the area again just before you pour; make the soil moist but not muddy. Oil the inside of the forms to make them easier to remove after the concrete sets.

2 Pouring and Spreading the Concrete. You'll need at least one helper to pour and spread the concrete. Spread it with a rake or hoe, compacting it gently into the footing areas. Use a shovel to move concrete into the footing trench. As you pour, use the tines of the rake to pull up the reinforcing mesh so that it is roughly centered, vertically, in the slab.

Make the pour to about 1 inch above the forms to allow for settling. Use a long 2x4 to screed (level) the concrete. Move the board in a side-to-side motion as you pull it toward you.

3 Finishing the Surface. Tamp the concrete with a concrete tamper, then smooth it with a bull float. The tools you use to finish the slab depend on the surface you want. A wooden float or trowel produces a rough, skid-proof finish. After floating the concrete, move the trowel freely in a series of arcs. A metal trowel produces a slick, smooth finish with a process known as "slick troweling." It takes some practice and is beyond the scope of this book. For details, see the Patios & Walks Quick Guide. A broom finish is yet another option; after floating, drag a stiff-bristle shop broom over the surface to create a slightly ridged

surface. Install anchor bolts for the mudsill while the concrete is still wet. Allow the concrete to cure fully (seven to ten days) before attaching the mudsills.

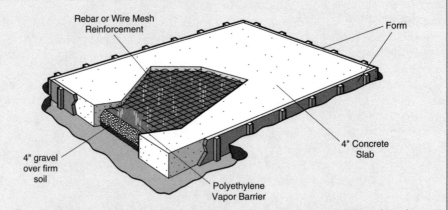

Rebar or Wire Mesh Reinforcement

Form

4" gravel over firm soil

4" Concrete Slab

Polyethylene Vapor Barrier

1 Backfill excavation with gravel; install vapor barrier. Then lay down wire mesh reinforcement or rebar, suspended an inch or two above the vapor barrier.

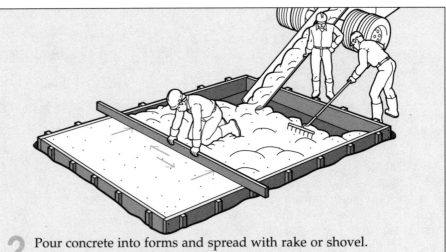

2 Pour concrete into forms and spread with rake or shovel. Use a long 2×4 to screed concrete level.

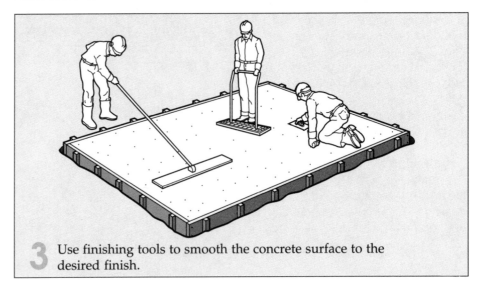

3 Use finishing tools to smooth the concrete surface to the desired finish.

F R A M I N G

This chapter covers conventional techniques for framing the shed floor, walls, and roof; you can adapt these to your particular design. The section on roof framing provides details for the three basic roof styles discussed in the first chapter—shed roof, gable roof, and barn-style roof. Specific plans for these three shed styles, plus a lean-to shed, follow this chapter.

Framing the Floor

Unless your shed has a poured-concrete slab, you'll need to frame the floor with conventional lumber. Most wood-frame floors use a technique called platform framing, which employs beams or header joists, stringer joists, and intermediate joists covered by sheets of plywood to form a platform. The rest of the shed structure is framed on top of it.

There are several variations of platform framing, shown on these pages. The method you use will depend on both the type of foundation you've installed (piers or a poured-concrete perimeter foundation) and the desired height of the floor above ground. Use pressure-treated lumber for beams, joists, and other floor-framing members.

As a rule, joists are 2×6s spaced 16 or 24 inches on center, depending on the load the floor must support. Typically, they run parallel to the short dimension of the shed (for example, the 8-foot dimension of an 8×10 shed). If the shed is 8 feet wide or less, the joists can span the full width of the building without any intermediate supports; however, blocking will be required to help strengthen the joists and provide nailing surfaces for plywood flooring or subflooring.

For sheds 10 to 12 feet wide, support the joists midspan with a girder attached to posts or piers. For larger buildings, 2×8 or 2×10 joists may be necessary. Check local building codes for required sizes, spans, and spacings of floor-framing members.

Basic Framing Techniques

Pier Foundations. With a precast pier foundation, you generally attach the beams or joists directly to the piers to keep the floor level and as low as possible. If for some reason you want to elevate the floor (or part of it) more than a foot or so above ground, such as when building the shed on a sloping lot, attach 4x4 posts to the piers (using metal connectors), then attach the beams to the posts. Otherwise, you can use one of three methods:

■ *Doubled Header.* Nail a doubled header directly to the pier blocks on each long side of the shed (use 16d galvanized nails), then hang intermediate joists between the header joists with joist hangers. The two end joists, or stringer joists, are nailed to the ends of the doubled header joist at each corner with 16d galvanized nails, as shown.

■ *4×6 Beams.* Instead of using doubled header joists, attach 4×6 beams to the piers with 20d galvanized nails or the appropriate metal connectors, then hang the joists between them as you would for a doubled header.

■ *Header on Beam.* Attach beams directly to the pier blocks with 20d galvanized nails or metal connectors, running the long dimension of the building. Attach header joists, stringer joists, and intermediate joists to the top of the beams with 10d galvanized nails, as shown.

Perimeter Foundations. The method for attaching joists to a concrete perimeter foundation is similar to method for a header on beam above, except that you toenail the stringer and header joists to the mudsills anchored to the foundation, then attach the intermediate joists, as shown.

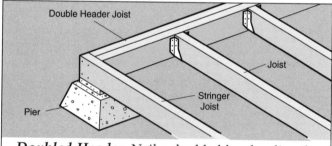

Doubled Header. Nail a doubled header directly to the pier blocks.

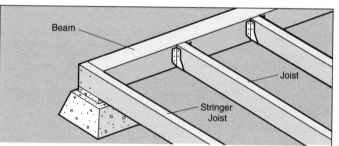

4×6 Beam. Instead of a doubled header, you can use a 4×6 beam nailed to the piers.

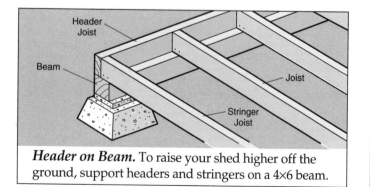

Header on Beam. To raise your shed higher off the ground, support headers and stringers on a 4×6 beam.

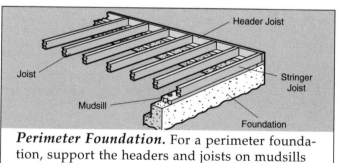

Perimeter Foundation. For a perimeter foundation, support the headers and joists on mudsills bolted to the foundation.

Framing Sequence

1 Cutting and Positioning the Framing Members. Cut the beams (if you're using these), stringer joists, and header joists to length. Attach the beams to the piers with 20d nails or metal connectors. Then toenail the header and stringer joists to the top of the beams with 10d nails, as shown (if you're hanging joists between the beams, omit this step). Be sure to place all framing members crown side up. To do this, sight along the edge of the board. If you notice a curve, make sure the convex side is up. If beams aren't used, toenail the header joists and stringer joists directly to the piers or mudsills (for perimeter foundations) with 16d galvanized nails. Connect the stringer joists to the doubled header joists at each corner with four 16d galvanized nails, as shown.

2 Squaring and Leveling the Joists. Square the header and stringer joists by measuring opposite diagonals and double-checking each corner with a framing square. Toenail the joists to the piers, beams, or mudsills with 10d galvanized nails. If necessary, drive cedar shims under the beams and joists to level them.

3 Marking Joist Locations. Starting at one corner, measure along one header joist 16 or 24 inches, then mark lines across the top and on both sides of the joist at this point. Mark an X beyond each line to indicate on which side of it to place the joist. Mark the opposite header joist in the same manner, starting at the same end of the building. If you're hanging joists between the beams, mark both end beams and any intermediate beams in the same manner.

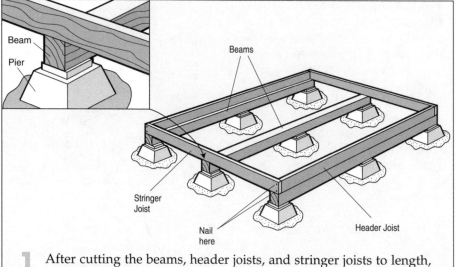

1 After cutting the beams, header joists, and stringer joists to length, place them on top of the piers and nail them together at the corners.

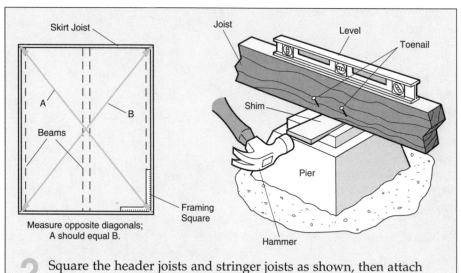

Measure opposite diagonals; A should equal B.

2 Square the header joists and stringer joists as shown, then attach them to piers, shimming to level if needed.

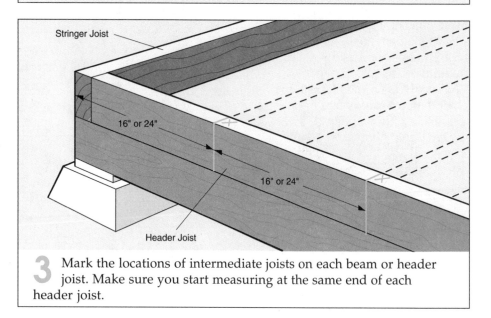

3 Mark the locations of intermediate joists on each beam or header joist. Make sure you start measuring at the same end of each header joist.

4 Squaring and Attaching the Joists. Use 16d galvanized nails to end-nail the joists to the header joists where marked in Step 3, then toenail them to the beams or mudsills with 10d galvanized nails. You can make a stronger connection by using joist hangers and hurricane ties for this purpose; see Metal Connectors, page 18. Use a framing square to check that each joist is installed at right angles to the header joists.

5 Hanging Joists between the Beams. If the ends of the intermediate joists aren't supported by a beam or mudsill (in other words, if you're hanging the joists between the beams), use metal joist hangers, as shown.

6 Installing Blocking and Bridging. If necessary, install 2×4 blocking between the joists to support the edges of the plywood floor panels. If the joists are 2×6 or wider and are longer than 8 feet, install blocking of the same width or cross-bridging at midspan to keep the joists from twisting. The cross-bridging can be 1×4s or 2×2s with mitered ends, or metal bridging (available at lumberyards).

7 Laying Plywood Flooring. Use 8d spiral or annular ring nails to attach the plywood subflooring to the joists, spacing nails every 8 inches around the panel perimeter and every 12 inches across the face. Orient the panels so the long dimension runs across the joists. If the floor is wider than 8 feet, arrange the panels so the joints are staggered, as shown. Use a portable circular saw or hand saw to trim off any overhanging plywood edges.

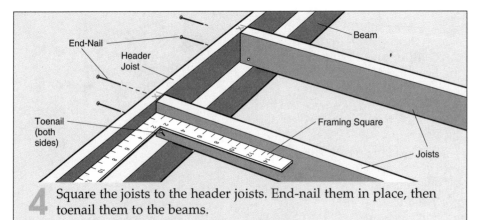

4 Square the joists to the header joists. End-nail them in place, then toenail them to the beams.

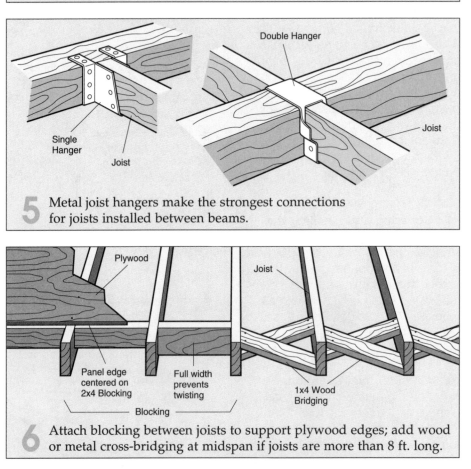

5 Metal joist hangers make the strongest connections for joists installed between beams.

6 Attach blocking between joists to support plywood edges; add wood or metal cross-bridging at midspan if joists are more than 8 ft. long.

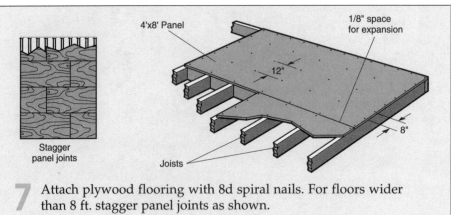

7 Attach plywood flooring with 8d spiral nails. For floors wider than 8 ft. stagger panel joints as shown.

If you're building a shed attached to the house or another existing building, your design may require you to attach one or more ledgers to the house wall. Generally, you would attach a horizontal ledger to the wall where it meets the shed roof, then attach the shed rafters to the ledger. The framing details for this procedure are shown on pages 51–53.

Depending on the floor height of the shed, you may also need to attach a ledger near the bottom of the house wall to support the shed's floor joists where they meet the house. The ledger takes the place of one of the header joists; the other three sides of the floor are framed as shown on the preceding pages. The drawings below

and on the next page show several methods of attaching ledgers.

If the house has a masonry wall, or if you're attaching the floor ledger to the concrete foundation of the house, use lag screws and expansion shields, or stud anchors, as shown in the drawings below. After marking the joist locations on the face of the ledger, drill holes in the ledger for stud anchors or expansion shields. The holes should be no more than 24 inches apart and should not fall on joist locations. Hold the ledger against the wall at the appropriate height. Keep it in place with temporary 2×4 braces with cleats. Check that the ledger is level, and use the holes in it as guides to drill holes into the house wall with a masonry

bit. Remove the ledger and install expansion shields. Secure the ledger with lag screws or drill holes through the ledger and into the wall, then drive stud anchors in place. With stud anchors, secure the ledger with washers and nuts, as shown. Check the level of the ledger again as you tighten bolts or screws with a wrench. If necessary, loosen the connectors and adjust the ledger. The ledger for the shed roof can be attached by the same methods or by shooting 10d concrete nails through the ledger into the wall with a pneumatic nailer or .22-caliber cartridge-type nail gun. A heavy bead of construction adhesive applied to the backside of the ledger will provide additional holding power and help prevent leaks.

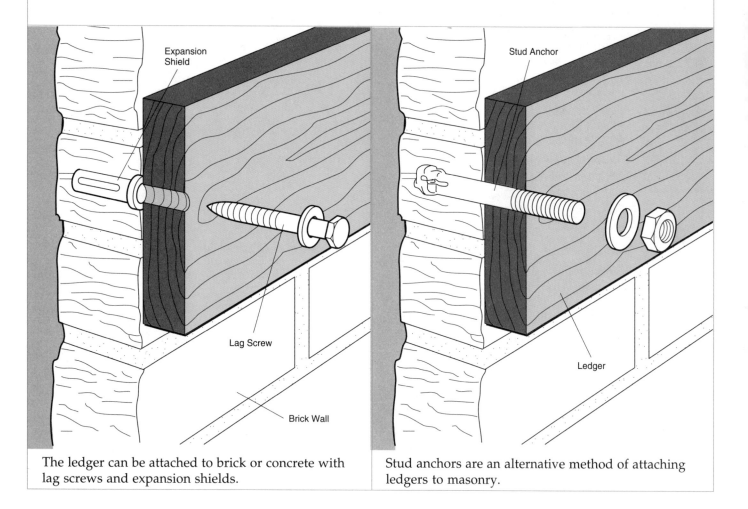

The ledger can be attached to brick or concrete with lag screws and expansion shields.

Stud anchors are an alternative method of attaching ledgers to masonry.

When attaching ledgers to wood, the ledger for the shed floor should be securely fastened to the floor header of the house and not to the studs or siding. Similarly, you should attach the roof ledger to the top plates of the house wall framing, if possible; otherwise, attach it to the studs. To locate the floor header or top plates from the out-side of the house, find the inside floor or ceiling level by measuring up or down from an inside window sill and transferring the measurement to the outside wall. For floor ledgers, measure down another 6 inches or more; this will be the approximate center of the floor header. Brace the ledger up against the header or mark on the outside wall; tack it in place with nails, if possible, making sure it is level. Then install lag screws no more than 24 inches apart. You'll need to drill pilot holes for the screws; use a bit with a slightly smaller diameter than that of the screw threads. If the house has stucco siding, you'll need a masonry bit to drill through it and into the header.

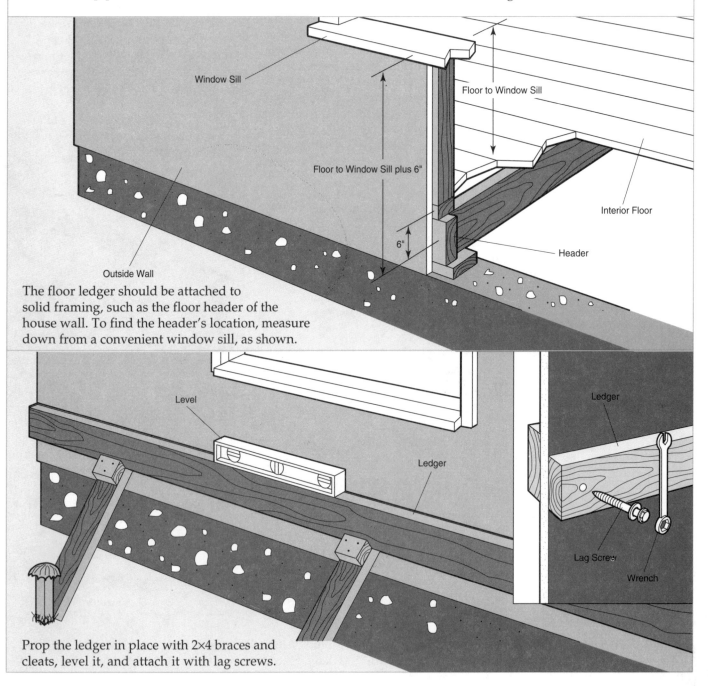

The floor ledger should be attached to solid framing, such as the floor header of the house wall. To find the header's location, measure down from a convenient window sill, as shown.

Prop the ledger in place with 2×4 braces and cleats, level it, and attach it with lag screws.

Framing the Walls

The walls are framed with 2×4 sole plates, studs, and double top plates. Rough openings for windows and doors include jack studs (also called trimmer studs), cripples, and headers. Windows include sills as well. Studs are spaced on 16- or 24-inch centers; cripples above doors and windows should maintain this spacing. On sheds 10 by 12 feet or larger, it's a good idea to nail 1×4 diagonal bracing to the inside of the wall framing to keep the walls from racking; bracing is required for board-type siding, whether it be of wood, vinyl, or aluminum. You'll also need to install nailing blocks or strapping if you're using vertical board siding (see page 62).

Before you start framing the walls, determine the size and location of the rough openings for doors and windows. If you're installing a pre-hung door or manufactured windows, use the rough opening size given in the instructions that come with the unit. If you're making your own doors or windows, first choose a rough opening size that suits you, then build the door or window to fit it.

Each long wall is framed to equal the overall length of the building, with two studs separated by spacers at each end to form corner posts, as shown. The two shorter walls are framed to fit between the two long walls; that is, they will be 7 inches shorter than the overall width of the building. They have a single stud at each end and

meet the long walls at each corner as shown in the inset below.

To avoid framing mistakes during construction, you can make an elevation drawing of each wall, showing the sizes and spacing of various framing members. If you've chosen to make a shed-roof shed, the tops of the studs and the ends of the top plates must be cut at an angle to build the sloping side walls (see pages 48–49).

It's easiest if you frame each wall on the ground (or on the floor platform), then lift it into position and brace it. Keep in mind you'll need a helper to muscle the wall into place.

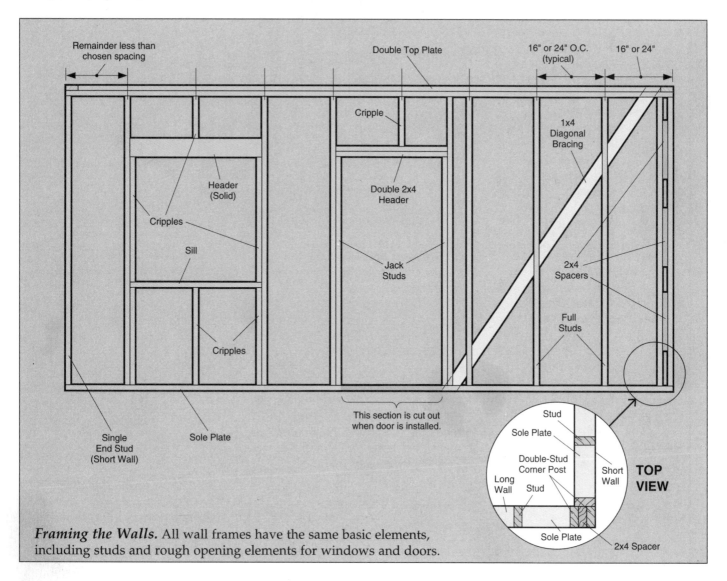

Framing the Walls. All wall frames have the same basic elements, including studs and rough opening elements for windows and doors.

Framing Sequence

1 Marking the Sole Plate and Top Plate. Start with one of the long walls. Cut the sole plate and one of the top plates to the full length of the floor platform or mudsill (both plates should be exactly the same length). Determine the location of full studs, jack studs (for door openings), and cripples (for door and window openings), then measure and mark both the top and bottom plates for these wall-framing members.

2 Assembling the Wall. Frame the corner posts for the long walls as shown. Align these and all full studs on the marks and drive two 16d nails through the top and sole plates into each end of the studs. Install jack studs and end cripples for window openings by face-nailing them to full studs with 8d nails, spaced 12 inches apart. Then install the headers and sills by driving 16d nails through adjacent full studs into the header/sill ends; toenail the headers to the jack studs with two 8d nails. Use 4×4 headers for openings up to 3 feet wide; header sizes for larger openings are dictated by local codes. Install cripples by toenailing them into the header, top plate, and bottom plate with 8d nails.

3 Lifting the Wall into Place. With a helper, lift the framed wall into place. Use short 1×4 blocks attached to the header joist or mudsill, as shown, to align the sole plate with the outside edge of the platform. Using a level, plumb the wall while a helper attaches the 1×4 braces, as shown. Drive two 16d nails through the sole plate into the floor or mudsill between each stud. Do not nail the sole plate within the door opening, as it will be cut out later when you install the door.

4 Building and Erecting the Remaining Walls. Frame, erect, and brace the opposite long wall, then the two side walls (steps 1 through 3), and attach them to the floor in the same manner. Connect all four walls at the corners by driving 16d nails at 12-inch intervals through the end studs of the short walls and into the corner posts of the long walls. To complete the framing, add the second top plates (called cap plates). Overlap the plates, as shown, to reinforce the corners.

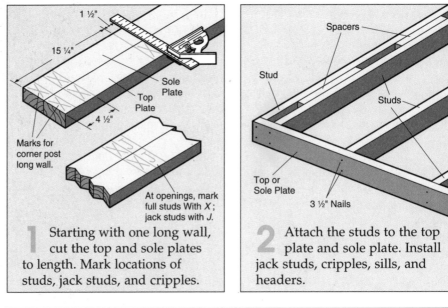

1 Starting with one long wall, cut the top and sole plates to length. Mark locations of studs, jack studs, and cripples.

2 Attach the studs to the top plate and sole plate. Install jack studs, cripples, sills, and headers.

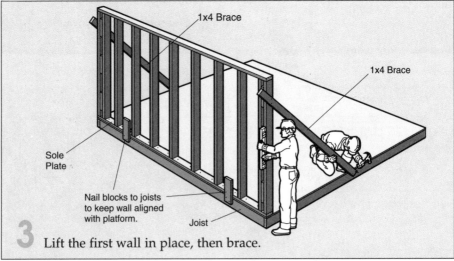

3 Lift the first wall in place, then brace.

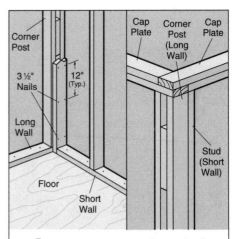

4 Frame, erect, and attach the opposite long wall, then the two side walls. Connect the four walls at each corner, then add the second top (cap) plates.

Framing the Roof

Roof framing takes a bit more skill than framing the floor and walls because you need to cut rafter ends at an angle and notch them to fit over the top plates of the walls. Before you start, determine the slope or pitch of the roof. Steep-pitched roofs require longer rafters, and therefore more lumber, but provide more headroom and are better suited in cold climates where the roof must shed heavy snow loads. Lower-pitched roofs are suitable in warm climates.

Roof pitch is expressed as a ratio of the rafter's vertical rise to its horizontal run. On a gable roof, for instance, the total rise is the measurement from the top plate to the roof peak; the total run is one-half the width, or span, of the shed. Once you know the total run and rise, you can calculate the pitch, and vice versa. For example, if the rafter rises 6 inches for every 12 inches of run, the pitch is 6 in 12.

A 3-in-12 pitch is the minimum recommended for installing asphalt or wood shingles; for lower pitches, use asphalt roll roofing with sealed joints. A pitch of 6 in 12 or steeper is recommended in areas subject to heavy snow loads.

After you've determined the roof style (pages 6–7) and the roof pitch you want, decide how much overhang to allow at the eaves and gable ends. This will determine the overall length of the rafters. Rafters are typically 2×4s or 2×6s spaced on 24-inch centers. The following pages provide specific framing details for the three basic roof types discussed in this book, shed, gable, and gambrel or barn-style.

Rafter Layout: Shed Roof

The shed roof is easiest to frame; simply run continuous rafters between the taller front wall and shorter back wall. Notches, called bird's-mouths, are cut into the rafters where they intersect the walls. Generally, you can use 2×4 rafters for sheds up to 8 feet wide; use 2×6s for wider sheds. For details on framing the slanted side walls, see pages 48–49.

1 **Measuring and Cutting the Rafters.** After erecting all four walls, measure the length of the slanting top edge of the side walls. To this dimension, add the desired amount of overhang at the front and back of the shed (typically 12 to 18 inches). Cut the rafters to this length.

For an 8-foot-wide shed with a front wall 2 feet taller than the back wall, 12-foot-long rafters provide about 18 inches of overhang at the front and back walls. The pitch, in this case, would be 3 in 12.

2 **Marking Bird's Mouth Cuts.** Select a straight rafter from the ones just cut. Position the rafter across the front and back walls just inside the top plate of one of the side walls, with the desired amount of overhang at each end, as shown. Then, use a square and mark the rafter for bird's-mouth cuts where it intersects the front and back walls. Make the cuts 1½ inches deep where the rafters will meet the inside of the walls as shown in the drawing.

3 **Cutting Bird's-Mouths.** Re move the rafter and cut out the bird's mouths at the marks. Test the rafter for fit against the front and back top plates; when dropped into position, the rafter's bottom edge

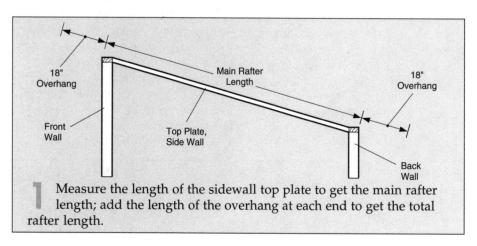

1 Measure the length of the sidewall top plate to get the main rafter length; add the length of the overhang at each end to get the total rafter length.

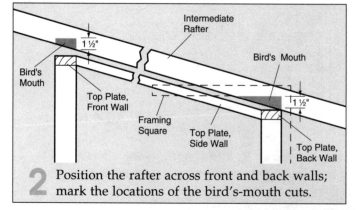

2 Position the rafter across front and back walls; mark the locations of the bird's-mouth cuts.

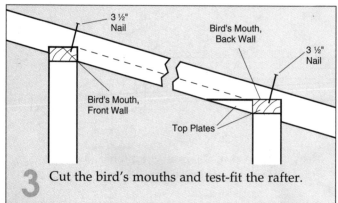

3 Cut the bird's mouths and test-fit the rafter.

should align perfectly with the bottom edge of the sidewall top plate. If it does, use this rafter as a template to cut bird's mouths for all of the rafters except the two end ones.

4 Attaching the Rafters. Use 16d nails to attach each end rafter (without bird's-mouth cuts) to the outside edge of each slanted top plate, so that the bottom edge of the rafter is flush with the bottom edge of the top plate. Then attach the intermediate rafters on 24-inch centers between the end rafters by driving a single 16d nail through the top of each rafter into the plate, over the bird's-mouth cuts. After the rafters are in place, install sheathing (page 60) and fascia (page 76).

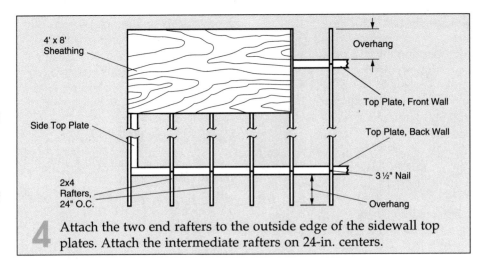

4 Attach the two end rafters to the outside edge of the sidewall top plates. Attach the intermediate rafters on 24-in. centers.

Rafter Layout: Gable Roof

For gable roofs, you can either run the rafters individually to a center ridge board or assemble gable-style roof trusses on the ground and lift them into position. Both methods are described on the following pages. Some lumberyards also carry prefabricated trusses for larger roof spans. While more expensive than framing with individual components or making your own trusses, prefab trusses can save you hours of measuring, marking, cutting, and assembling

roof components. Consider them if you will be building a large shed.

If you're framing rafters individually, bird's-mouth cuts are made near the bottom end of each rafter where it intersects the top plate of the wall. Depending on the rafter length and roof pitch (usually on sheds over 8 feet wide), you may need to add collar ties to reinforce the rafters. In buildings without ceiling joists, collar ties keep the rafters from forcing the walls outward. These ties are usually 1×4s or 1×6s attached between each set of rafters midway between the roof peak and the top plate of the wall, as shown in the drawing at bottom right, page 42. Whether using trusses or rafters, you must frame in

the overhang at the gable ends before installing the roof sheathing.

Determining Rafter Length. The easiest way to lay out a rafter is by stepping it off with a framing square, as shown on page 39. But first, you'll need to know approximately how long the rafters will be so you can order lumber. The following example shows how to calculate the rafter length for an 8-foot-wide shed with a 6-in-12 pitch and a 12-inch overhang. A bit of simple math tells you that if the total run is 4 feet (one-half the shed width measured from the center of the top plate to one outside edge), the total rise will be 2 feet (measured from the same center point on the top plate to the center-

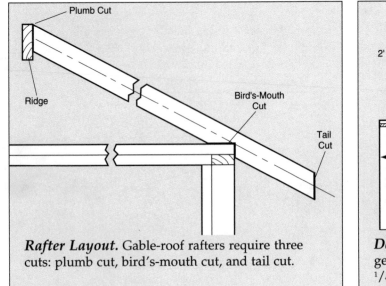

Rafter Layout. Gable-roof rafters require three cuts: plumb cut, bird's-mouth cut, and tail cut.

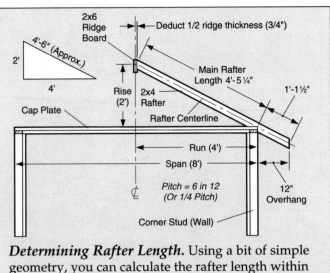

Determining Rafter Length. Using a bit of simple geometry, you can calculate the rafter length within 1/4 in. or so.

line of the rafter at the roof peak); on a 10-foot-wide shed the total run will be 5 feet and the rise 2½ feet.

To figure out what length rafter you need (within ¼ inch or so, for estimating purposes), either consult the tables on the face of your rafter square or do a bit of geometry. Think of the total rise as the vertical side of a right triangle, and the total run as the horizontal side, then calculate the hypotenuse. In this case, 2 feet squared + 4 feet squared equals 20 feet. The square root of 20 equals 4.472, or roughly 4 feet, 6 inches. From this figure, deduct one-half the ridge thickness (¾ inch) to get the main rafter length from the ridge to the outside edge of the building, or 4 feet, 5¼ inches. Use this same equation to determine the rafter length required for the 12-inch roof overhang (6 inches squared + 12 inches squared equals the rafter length squared, or roughly 1 foot, 1½ inches. Add this dimension to the overall rafter length to get 5 feet, 6¾ inches total rafter length. Then add about 1 inch to each end to allow for the angled plumb and tail cuts in the rafter. So, you'd cut the rafters from 6 footers. Your calculations needn't be precise, as you'll be taking exact measurements when you step off the rafters.

Stepping Off Rafters

To step off a rafter, you'll need a framing square. Once you've stepped off one rafter and marked the locations for the plumb cut, tail cut, and bird's-mouth cut, you can use it as a template to cut the rest.

1. Select a straight board for your rafter template. Position the framing square at the top end of the rafter where shown in the drawing, aligning the 6-inch mark on the tongue (short leg) and the 12-inch mark on the body (long leg) with the top edge of the rafter. Mark a line on the rafter end along the tongue of the square. Then step off four 12-inch increments and mark the bottom end where shown on the drawing. If the rafter must be longer than the one in this example, step off one 12-inch increment for each foot of run. To change the roof pitch, use the inch mark on the tongue that corresponds to the rise (the 3-inch mark for a 3-in-12 pitch, for example).

2. The last mark you made (Step 1) indicates where the rafter intersects the outer edge of the wall. Flip the square over and mark the location of the bird's mouth and tail cut. Then move the framing square back to the top end of the rafter, deduct one-half the ridge thickness, as shown, and mark the plumb cut. Cut the rafter at these marks (plumb cut, bird's mouth, and tail cut).

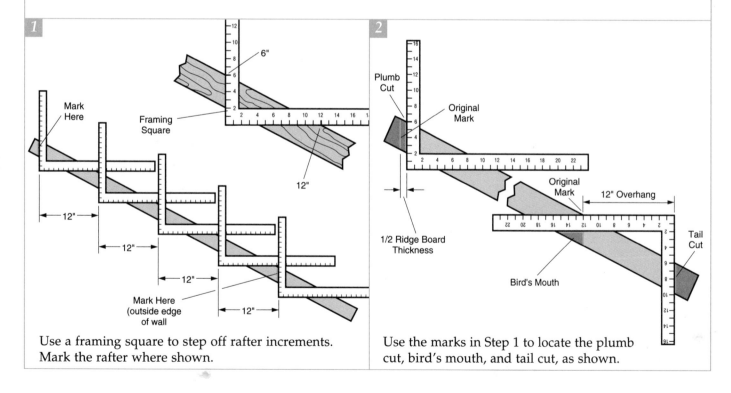

Use a framing square to step off rafter increments. Mark the rafter where shown.

Use the marks in Step 1 to locate the plumb cut, bird's mouth, and tail cut, as shown.

Framing Sequence for Gable Roof

1 Cutting the Rafters. After you lay out and cut a first rafter, use it as a template to lay out a second. Test the two rafters for fit on the ground by placing the bird's mouths over the end of a 2×4 cut to a length equal to the width of the shed measured across the top plate. Then place the top ends of the rafters against a block the thickness of the ridge board. After making any necessary adjustments to the cuts, use either rafter as a template to cut the rest.

2 Marking the Ridge Board and Top Plates. Cut the ridge board to length and mark the rafter positions on it and on the top plates. If the roof will overhang at the gable ends, allow for the overhang at each end when you cut the ridge board (see gable-end detail, page 43).

3 Raising the End Rafters. On the ground, attach two end rafters to the ridge board; end-nail through the ridge board into the first rafter with 16d nails; then toe-nail the opposite rafter to the board with 10d nails. Adjust the rafter spread until the distance between the bird's-mouth cuts matches the exact length of the top plate, then nail a temporary cleat to hold the rafters in this position.

4 Adding the Remaining Rafters and Collar Ties. Attach a temporary brace to the opposite wall to support the other end of the ridge board. Then, with one or two helpers, lift this assembly into position. Nail the end rafters to the plate, then level the ridge board and tack it to the temporary support at the opposite end. Fill in the remaining rafters, frame in the gable end supports, then attach the collar ties. If you're installing ceiling joists, nail these in place before erecting the rafters; you can then tack a sheet of $5/8$-inch plywood over the joists as a platform to stand on while framing the rafters. Where the rafters intersect the wall, nail them to both the top plate and to any adjoining joists. Finally, cut and install short blocks between the rafters where they intersect the top plate. This is called bird blocking; it is used to fill the open space between the top plate and the roof sheathing between the rafters.

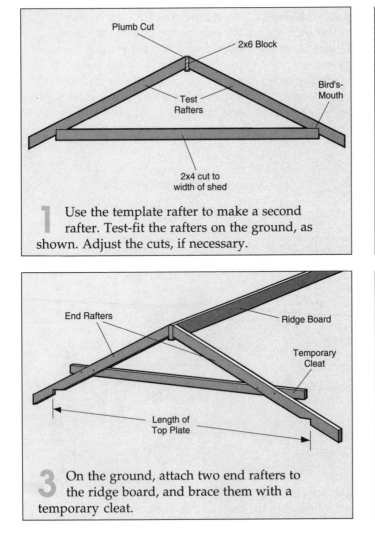

1 Use the template rafter to make a second rafter. Test-fit the rafters on the ground, as shown. Adjust the cuts, if necessary.

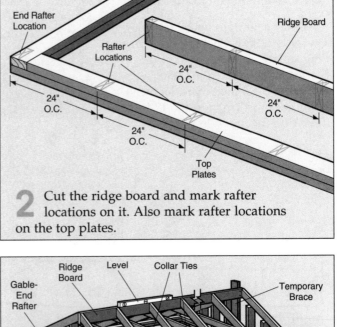

2 Cut the ridge board and mark rafter locations on it. Also mark rafter locations on the top plates.

3 On the ground, attach two end rafters to the ridge board, and brace them with a temporary cleat.

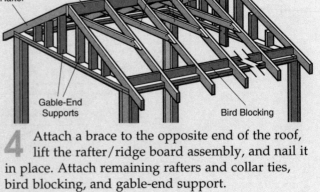

4 Attach a brace to the opposite end of the roof, lift the rafter/ridge board assembly, and nail it in place. Attach remaining rafters and collar ties, bird blocking, and gable-end support.

Here are two of the most common methods of framing in the gable ends. They allow you to create as little or as much overhang as you want.

Closing the Gable Ends. This style has no overhang at the gable ends. After framing in the rafters and applying the roof sheathing, run the wall sheathing or siding up to the top edges of the roof sheathing at the gable ends, then cover it with a 1×6 or 1×4 (called a rake board), as shown.

Creating a Gable Overhang. To provide greater weather protection, the ridge board is extended past the end wall to the desired width of the overhang, then a set of barge or verge rafters is attached to the end of the ridge and to the rafters with short 2×4 blocks, called outriggers or ladders. The roof sheathing extends flush to the outside edge of the barge rafters.

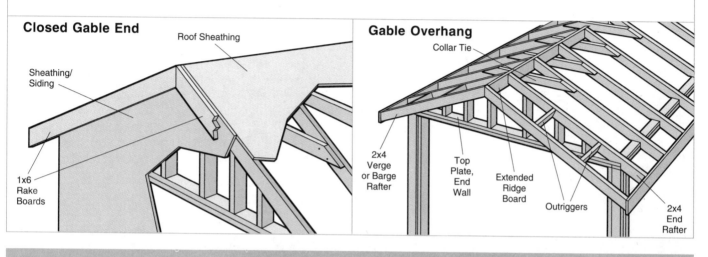

Closed Gable End
Roof Sheathing
Sheathing/ Siding
1x6 Rake Boards

Gable Overhang
Collar Tie
2x4 Verge or Barge Rafter
Top Plate, End Wall
Extended Ridge Board
Outriggers
2x4 End Rafter

To finish the roof framing, install the subfascia, soffit nailers, fascia, and soffits as shown on the drawing. If you're installing aluminum or vinyl fascia and soffits, refer to the instructions that come with these materials.

The following lumber sizes assume you've used 2×4 rafters. First, nail the 1×4 subfascia to the ends of the roof outriggers and rafter ends along the eaves. (The 1×4 subfascia and 1×6 fascia along the eaves must be lowered slightly to accommodate the slope of the roof sheathing, as shown.) Then install the 1×4 eaves soffit nailer and 2×2 gable soffit nailer, making sure they are level with the bottom edge of the subfascia. Nail the 1×6 fascia into place, then nail the 1/2-inch plywood soffit to the bottom edge of the subfascia and soffit nailers.

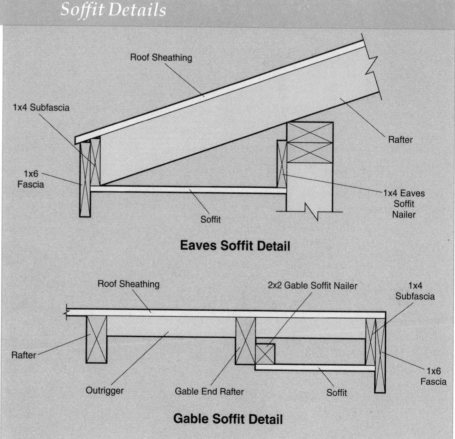

Roof Sheathing
1x4 Subfascia
1x6 Fascia
Rafter
1x4 Eaves Soffit Nailer
Soffit

Eaves Soffit Detail

Roof Sheathing
2x2 Gable Soffit Nailer
1x4 Subfascia
Rafter
Outrigger
Gable End Rafter
Soffit
1x6 Fascia

Gable Soffit Detail

Installing Trusses

If you decide to use prefabricated trusses instead of framing your own rafters, the installation is as follows.

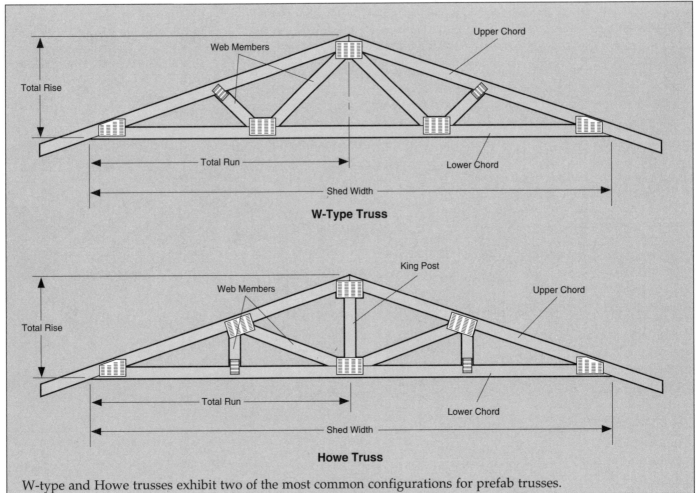

W-type and Howe trusses exhibit two of the most common configurations for prefab trusses.

1 Installing the First Truss.
Mark the truss positions on the top plates of the two side walls (trusses are spaced on 24-inch centers). With a helper, lift the front truss and position it on the first set of marks, directly above one of the end walls (if you want overhang at the gable ends, it's a good idea to sheathe the end trusses and notch them for outriggers before raising). Adjust to provide equal overhang at each side. Attach the truss to the end wall by toenailing through the lower chord of the truss into the top plate.

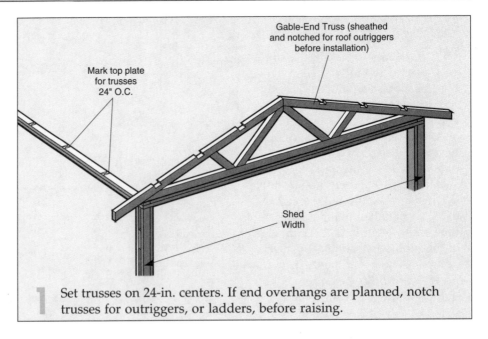

1 Set trusses on 24-in. centers. If end overhangs are planned, notch trusses for outriggers, or ladders, before raising.

2 Attaching the Remaining Trusses.

Repeat Step 1 for the other gable end. Once the gable end trusses are installed, run a taut string from the peak of one gable-end truss to the other. Use the string as a guide to align the peaks of the interior trusses. Install these by nailing through the lower chords of the trusses into the top plates of the side walls at the marks. Connect the trusses at the center by nailing a 1×4 truss tie across the lower chords, as shown at top right.

3 Installing the Outriggers.

Install the 2×4 outriggers or roof ladders (if your plan calls for them) to the gable ends, as shown. You can vary the length of the outriggers depending on how much overhang you want. Typically, a 12- to 16-inch overhang is sufficient. If using a 16-inch overhang as shown at bottom right, cut the outriggers to 38½ inches. Cut notches into the end trusses (if you didn't do this before installation), then fit the outriggers into the notches cut into the top chords of the gable ends, butted up against the second truss. Attach them to both trusses with 16d nails where shown. Then add the 1×4 subfascia and 1×6 fascia. Repeat at the opposite end of the roof. If you desire a closed gable end, install the sheathing and rake board as shown on page 43 (as with conventional gable-roof framing, soffits can be added, if desired, as shown on the same page).

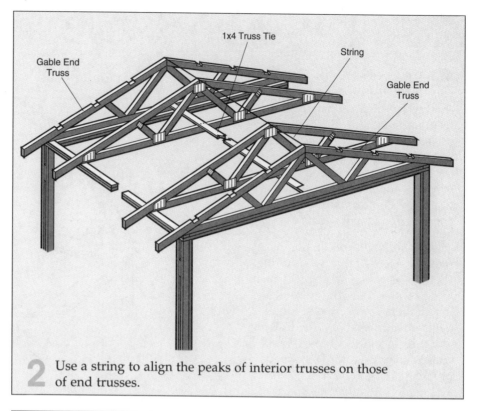

2 Use a string to align the peaks of interior trusses on those of end trusses.

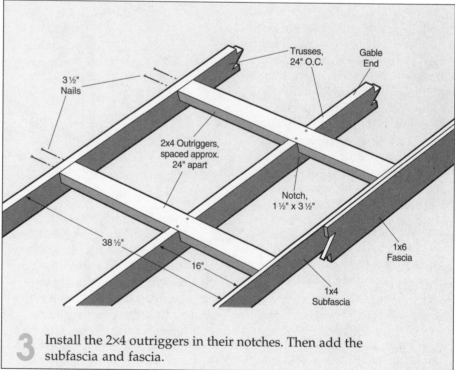

3 Install the 2×4 outriggers in their notches. Then add the subfascia and fascia.

Barn-style roofs have two pitches, usually 30 degrees from horizontal for the top pitch and 60 degrees from horizontal for the bottom pitch. Of course, these angles can be altered as you see fit. Framing for barn-style, or gambrel, roofs employs either truss construction (for large sheds or barns) or rib construction (small sheds).

Truss Construction. In this method, erect all four walls of the shed as described on page 38, then build or purchase roof trusses, and install them as you would for a gable-style truss roof. The drawing at top right shows a typical truss construction used for large sheds or barns (12 or more feet wide). The upper and lower chords are assembled on the ground, with plywood gussets. Permanent braces hold the gable-end trusses in position; you may need to install temporary 1×4 braces across the interior trusses to hold them in position until the roof sheathing is applied. Otherwise, no interior bracing is required. Installation is similar to that of gable-style trusses (pages 44–45). Depending on the width of the building, use 2×4s or 2×6s for the trusses; consult your local building department for details.

Rib Construction. This method, used for building barn-style sheds 10 feet wide or less, involves constructing complete framing units called ribs. These are similar to trusses, except that they include not only the roof members, but wall studs and floor joists as well. Studs are added to the rear wall rib (to provide a nailing surface for sheathing and siding), and a door is framed into the front wall rib. Plywood wall sheathing holds the front and rear ribs together; the interior wall ribs are reinforced with plywood gussets. The draw-

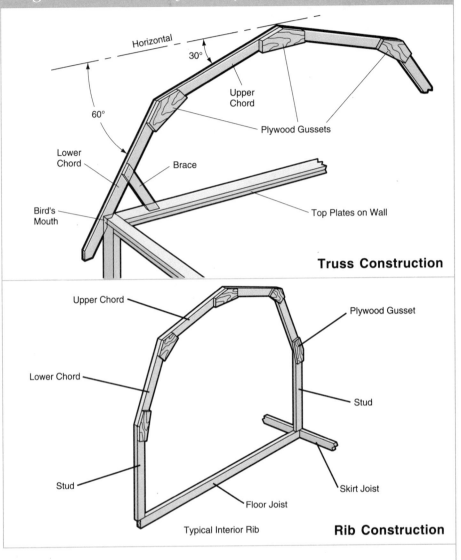

Truss Construction

Rib Construction

ing above shows a typical interior rib; pages 56–57 provide specific rib details for 8- and 10-foot-wide barn-style sheds. The length of the shed depends on how many interior ribs, spaced 24 inches on center, you use. The ribs require no additional bracing because the roof sheathing and wall sheathing hold the entire structure together.

If you use rib construction, bear in mind that the rib floor joists and stringer joists should be pressure-treated lumber. Also note that the structure should not sit directly on the ground. Either elevate it on

beams and concrete piers or attach it to mudsills (concrete foundations).

On large sheds and barns, or ones with conventional wall framing, assemble roof trusses on the ground, then lift them into position. Trusses are on 24-inch centers and are installed similarly to gable-style trusses.

Barn-style sheds 10 ft. wide or less often use 2×4 rib construction, as shown here. Each rib consists of roof members, studs, and floor joists; they are tied together at the bottom with stringer joists.

SHED PLANS

If you've read and become familiar with the preceding chapters on shed construction, you can apply your knowledge to building a shed from one of the four plans shown on the following pages. Each plan includes a materials list, detailed drawings, and step-by-step building instructions.

Shed-Roof Shed

The drawing at the bottom of this page shows a shed 8 feet wide by 8 feet long. The overall height of the front wall is 8 feet, and the back wall is 6 feet tall. Be sure to subtract the thickness of the top and bottom plates when cutting studs to length. Each of the four walls has a single top plate.

The materials list on the facing page does not include foundation materials (concrete footings, piers, beams, or concrete slab), windows, doors, sid-ing, or extra lumber for building steps or a ramp to the shed. Refer to appropriate sections of this book for options.

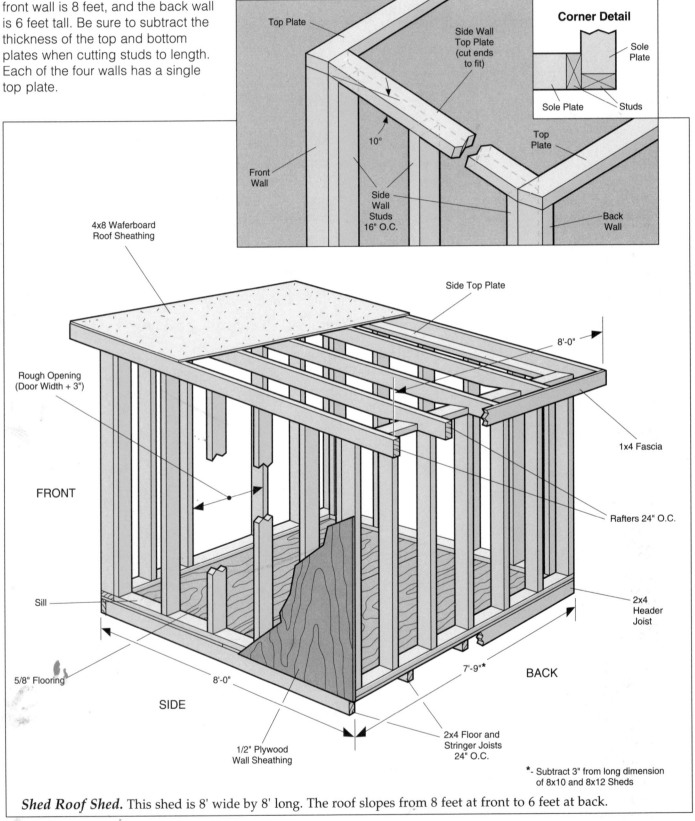

Corner Detail

Top Plate

Side Wall Top Plate (cut ends to fit)

Sole Plate

Sole Plate

Studs

10°

Front Wall

Side Wall Studs 16" O.C.

Top Plate

Back Wall

4x8 Waferboard Roof Sheathing

Side Top Plate

8'-0"

1x4 Fascia

Rough Opening (Door Width + 3")

Rafters 24" O.C.

FRONT

Sill

2x4 Header Joist

5/8" Flooring

8'-0"

7'-9"*

BACK

SIDE

1/2" Plywood Wall Sheathing

2x4 Floor and Stringer Joists 24" O.C.

*- Subtract 3" from long dimension of 8x10 and 8x12 Sheds

Shed Roof Shed. This shed is 8' wide by 8' long. The roof slopes from 8 feet at front to 6 feet at back.

1 Building the Floor Platform. Refer to the sections on Foundations (pages 20–30) and Framing the Floor (pages 32–34) for various options. Whether you choose a wood-frame floor or poured-concrete slab floor, the length of the finished floor platform and framing for the front and back walls is 3 inches shorter than the overall shed length (7 feet, 9 inches for an 8-foot-long shed, for example). This allows for the two 2x4 end rafters to be nailed to the outside of the top plate to accommodate 4x8-foot sheets of sheathing on the roof.

2 Erecting the Front and Back Walls. To assemble the 6-foot back wall, cut studs to 69 inches; for the 8-foot front wall, cut studs to 93 inches. Frame in the rough opening for the door (calculating by the door width plus 3 inches). See pages 37–38 for additional wall framing techniques.

3 Erecting the Side Walls. On both sides of the shed, measure between the sole plates of the front and back walls, then cut the side-wall sole plates to fit between them. Attach the sole plates, then cut and attach the side-wall end studs, as shown in the detail drawing (facing page). Cut the tops of the side-wall end studs and the ends of the top plate at a 10-degree angle to conform to the slope of the side wall. To do this, cut the pieces slightly longer than their finished length, then hold them in position. Use a T-bevel and pencil to transfer the angle to the top end of the studs and both ends of the top plate. Set your circular saw to make a 10-degree cut. Cut the single top plate to fit, then attach it to the end studs. Cut the remaining studs individually to fit between the top and bottom plates (on 16-inch centers). As shown in the drawing, the tops of the intermediate studs are also cut at a 10-degree angle. If desired, frame a rough window opening in one of the side walls at this time.

4 Installing the Roof. See pages 39–40 for rafter framing details. After installing the rafters, attach 1x4 fascia to the rafter ends, roof sheathing, and roof shingles. Bird blocking between the rafters is optional.

5 Finishing the Shed. Install wall sheathing (if used), siding, door, and windows (optional). Refer to the appropriate chapters in this book for installing these items. You'll find ideas on making your own door and windows on pages 71 and 73.

Materials List

8×8 SHED		8×10 SHED		8×12 SHED	
5	2×4 × 8' floor joists	6	2¹/₂4 × 8' floor joists	7	2×4 × 8' floor joists
2	2×4 × 8' headerjoists	2	2×4 × 10' header joists	2	2×4 × 12' header joists
8	2×4 × 8' sole/top plates	4	2×4 × 8' sole/top plates	4	2×4 × 8' sole/top plates
9	2×4 × 6' studs	4	2×4 × 10' sole/top plates	4	2×4 × 12' sole/top plates
16	2×4 × 8' studs	11	2×4 × 6' studs	12	2×4 × 6' studs
5	2×4 × 12' rafters	18	2×4 × 8' studs	19	2×4 × 8' studs
2	³/₄" plywood sheets (flooring)	6	2×4 × 12' rafters	7	2×4 × 12' rafters
3	⁷/₁₆" waferboard sheets (roof sheathing)	2¹/₂	³/₄" plywood sheets (flooring)	3	³/₄" plywood sheets (flooring)
2	1×4 × 8' pine or fir fascia	4	⁷/₁₆" waferboard sheets (roof sheathing)	4¹/₂	⁷/₁₆" waferboard sheets (roof sheathing)
8	¹/₂" plywood sheets (wall sheathing)	2	1×4 × 10' pine or fir fascia	2	1×4 × 12' pine or fir fascia
96 sq. ft.	roofing felt, shingles	9	¹/₂" plywood sheets (wall sheathing)	10	¹/₂" plywood sheets (wall sheathing)
1¹/₂ lbs.	16d nails	120 sq. ft.	roofing felt, shingles	144 sq. ft.	roofing felt, shingles
1 lb.	8d nails	2 lbs.	16d nails	2¹/₂ lbs.	16d nails
2¹/₂ lbs.	8d spiral nails (flooring, roof)	1¹/₂ lbs.	8d nails	2 lbs.	8d nails
2¹/₂ lbs.	6d galvanized nails (siding)	3 lbs.	8d spiral nails (flooring, roof)	3¹/₂ lbs.	8d spiral nails (flooring, roof)
1¹/₂ lbs.	1¹/₂" roofing nails.	3 lbs.	6d galvanized nails (siding)	3¹/₂ lbs.	6d galvanized nails (siding)
		2 lbs.	1¹/₂" roofing nails.	2¹/₂ lbs.	1¹/₂" roofing nails.

Attached Shed (Lean-To)

This small attached shed is perfect for storing a variety of garden tools and implements. Although you can make the shed as long or as deep as you want, the dimensions shown here make best use of standard plywood and lumber sizes. Because the shed is only 2 feet deep, flooring and foundation requirements are minimal. The back of the floor is supported by a 2×4 ledger attached to the house; the front, by 4×4 pressure-treated posts set in concrete, like fence posts. You can substitute a poured concrete slab for the wood-framed floor shown here.

The back edge of the roof is attached to the house by means of a horizontal ledger; the shed side walls tie into the house via vertical ledger supports. We recommend 1/2-inch exterior plywood for the floor and roof sheathing, use plywood siding for the walls.

Attached (Lean-to) Shed. The lean-to shed can be built against your house or fence. It's perfect for storing garden tools.

Materials/Cutting List

1	2×4* × 5'9" floor ledger
2	4×4* × 3' posts
2	2×4* × 2' stringer joists
1	2×4* × 5'9" header joist
16	2×4* × 1'9" joists
2'×6'	1/2" ext. plywood (flooring)
2	2×4 × 7'8 1/2" ledger supports
1	2×4 × 6' roof ledger
1	2×4 × 5'5" front-wall top plate
1	2×4 × 1'10 1/2" side-wall top plate
1	2×4 × 7" cripple
2	2×4 × 1'9" side-wall bottom plate
2	2×4 × 6'8 1/2" side-wall end studs
2	2×4 × 6'8 1/2" front-wall end studs
2	2×4 × 5'2" (doubled header)
2	2×4 × 5'10 1/2" jack studs
2	2×4 × 1'9" side wall blocking
3	2×4 × 27" rafters
4	1/2" plywood siding (siding, doors)
2'6"×6'4"	1/2" ext. plywood sheet (roof sheathing)
1	12'6"×6'4" 1/2" ext. plywood sheet (roof sheathing)
1	1×4 × 6'1" fascia
1	1×4 × 4'11" threshold
1	1×4 × 6'1 1/2" skirt board, front wall
2	1×4 × 2' skirt board, side walls
2	90-lb. sacks ready-mix concrete, gravel
14 sq. ft.	roofing felt, shingles
1	hasp and lock (shed door)
2 lbs.	16d nails
2 lbs.	8d nails
2 lbs.	6d galvanized nails (siding, sheathing)
2 lbs.	4d roofing nails.
6	4" strap hinges or T-hinges

* Pressure-treated lumber

1 Building the Floor Platform.

Cut the floor ledger to the length shown on the drawing. Level it and attach it to the house wall so that the bottom edge is about 3 to 4 inches above ground level. See pages 35 and 36 for details on attaching ledgers to wood and masonry walls. Next, locate and dig footing holes for posts at the front corners of shed. Cut the posts to length (add the depth below ground to the height above ground), then set them loosely in the holes (do not add concrete yet). Typically, posts should be set a minimum of 2 feet into the ground, and deeper in areas with severe frost heave.

Next, cut the two stringer joists and header joist to length. Attach the stringer joists to the post and ledger, then attach the header joist to the posts, as shown in the drawing at top right. The top edge of the joists should be flush with the post top. With a framing square and level, make the platform square and level by adjusting the post height and location in the hole and backfilling with gravel, while keeping the posts plumb. Carefully backfill the holes with concrete. Check again for level and square; make any minor adjustments while the concrete is still wet. After the concrete sets, install the two intermediate 2×4 joists and 1/2-inch plywood floor.

2 Attaching the Vertical Ledger Supports and Roof Ledger.

Cut the two vertical ledger supports to length and attach them to the house at the back corners of the floor platform. Use a level to plumb them vertically; the distance between the outside edges of the supports at the top should be exactly 6 feet. Attach the ledger supports to the house wall with 16d nails and construction adhesive (for wood siding) or power-driven concrete nails (for masonry siding). Cut the roof ledger to length and bevel the top edge at a 27-degree angle, as shown in the drawing at bottom right. Attach the roof ledger to the house wall, and toenail it into the ledger supports.

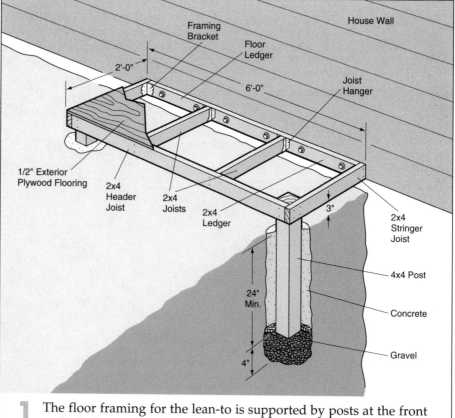

1 The floor framing for the lean-to is supported by posts at the front and a ledger attached to the house at the rear.

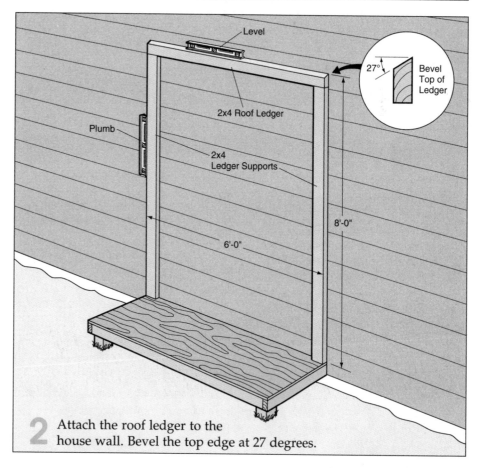

2 Attach the roof ledger to the house wall. Bevel the top edge at 27 degrees.

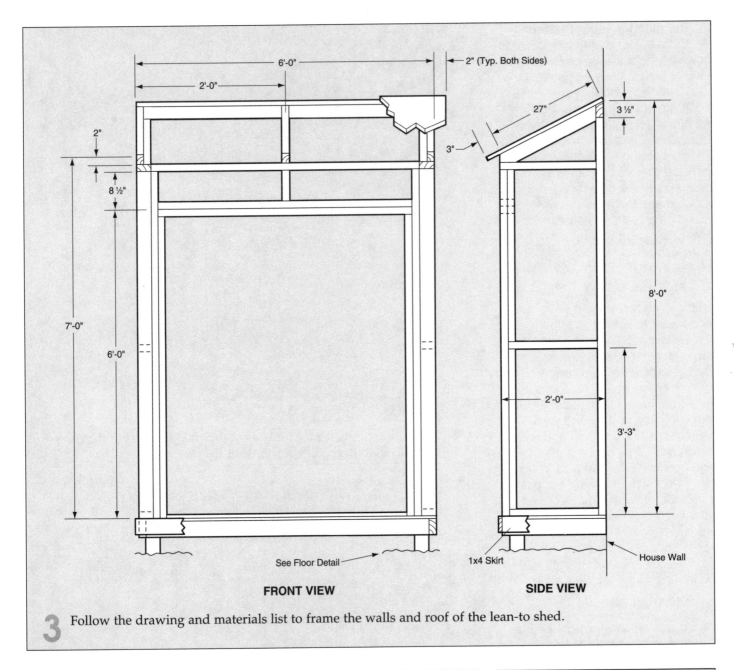

FRONT VIEW

SIDE VIEW

3 Follow the drawing and materials list to frame the walls and roof of the lean-to shed.

3 **Framing the Walls and Roof.**
Refer to the Framing Detail drawing on the facing pages. Cut all the framing pieces to the lengths indicated in the Materials/Cutting List on that page. Frame the side walls first, then attach the full studs, jack studs, top plate, header, and cripple to complete the front wall and door opening. Finally, cut and attach the rafters to the front-wall top plate and roof ledger.

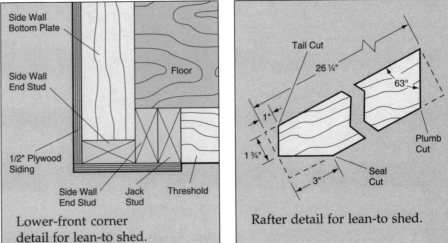

Lower-front corner detail for lean-to shed.

Rafter detail for lean-to shed.

4 **Installing the Siding, Roof Sheathing, and Roof.** Cut and attach the ¹⁄₂-inch plywood siding to the side walls, using 6d galvanized nails; then attach siding around the door opening in the front wall. The siding should be flush with the sides of the framed door opening and flush with the bottom edge of the top 2×4 in the doubled header. The bottom 2×4 in the header serves as a door stop.

Cut the roof sheathing so that it overlaps the front wall by 3 inches and the side walls by 2 inches. Using 8d galvanized finish nails, attach the 1×4 fascia board across the top of the front wall just under the roof overhang, as shown at top right, then install the 1×4 skirt around the base of the shed. As an option, you can install 1×4 trim strips to cover exposed plywood edges at the front corners of the shed, under the eaves on the side walls, and at the back corners of the shed where it meets the house wall.

Caulk the joint where the roof sheathing meets the house wall, and apply a metal drip cap to the front edge of the roof deck. Then cut and staple 15-pound roofing felt over the sheathing, and apply three-tab asphalt shingles or asphalt roll roofing. For more on roofing, see pages 60–61.

5 **Making and Hanging the Doors.** From ¹⁄₂-inch siding material, cut doors to the dimensions shown on the drawing at bottom right, or allow ¹⁄₁₆-inch clearance between each door and the rough opening (top, sides, and bottom) and a ¹⁄₈-inch gap where the two doors meet. Hang the doors with large strap hinges or T-hinges. For other options on making and hanging doors, see page 58.

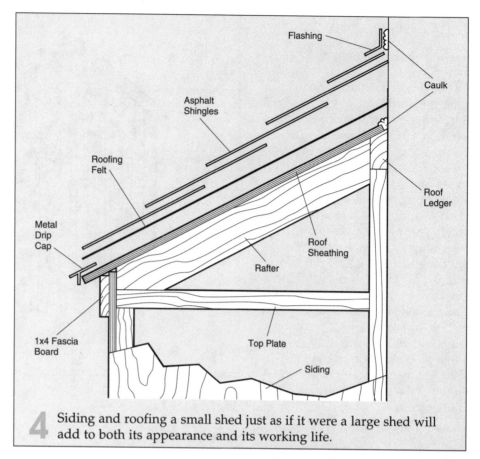

4 Siding and roofing a small shed just as if it were a large shed will add to both its appearance and its working life.

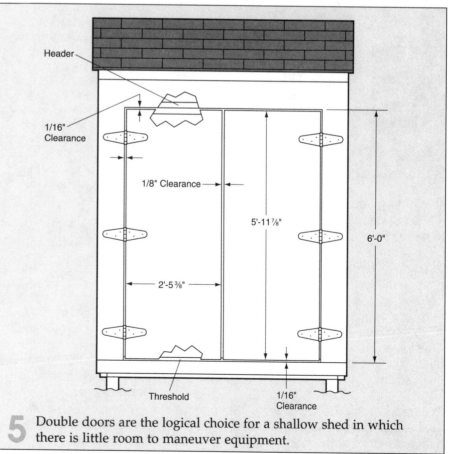

5 Double doors are the logical choice for a shallow shed in which there is little room to maneuver equipment.

Gable-Roof Shed

You can easily build a gable-roof shed of any size simply by following the framing sequence for floors, walls, and gable roofs (conventional or truss-type construction) in the previous chapter. These two pages show another way to frame this type of shed. Like the barn-style shed on pages 56 and 57, this shed uses simple rib construction. It consists of a front-wall rib, a rear-wall rib, and as many interior ribs as desired for the shed length you want, spaced on 2-foot centers. Each interior rib consists of two rafters, two studs, and a floor joist, reinforced with plywood gussets; the front- and rear-wall ribs include additional framing members as shown, and are made structurally stable by the plywood siding attached to them. The ribs are connected at the bottom with 2×4 stringer joists.

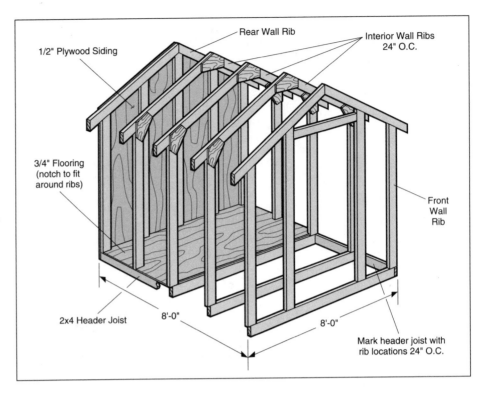

Rear Wall Rib

Interior Wall Ribs 24" O.C.

1/2" Plywood Siding

3/4" Flooring (notch to fit around ribs)

Front Wall Rib

2x4 Header Joist

8'-0"

8'-0"

Mark header joist with rib locations 24" O.C.

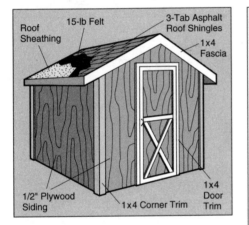

Roof Sheathing

15-lb Felt

3-Tab Asphalt Roof Shingles

1x4 Fascia

1x4 Door Trim

1/2" Plywood Siding

1x4 Corner Trim

Materials List

8×8 SHED		10×10 SHED	
2	2x4 × 8' header joists	2	2x4 × 10' stringer joists
1	2x4 front-wall rib assembly	1	2x4 front-wall rib assembly
1	2x4 rear-wall rib assembly	1	2x4 rear-wall rib assembly
3	2x4 interior-wall rib assemblies	4	2x4 interior-wall rib assemblies
2	$^3/_4$" plywood sheets (flooring)	$3^1/_4$	$^3/_4$" plywood sheets (flooring)
$2^1/_2$	$^7/_{16}$" waferboard sheets (roof sheathing)	4	$^7/_{16}$" waferboard sheets (roof sheathing)
4	1x4 × 10' pine or fir fascia/trim	2	1x4 × 10' pine or fir fascia/trim
2	1x4 × 14' pine or fir fascia/trim	4	1x4 × 14' pine or fir fascia/trim
$6^1/_2$	$^1/_2$" plywood siding (walls, door)	8	$^1/_2$" plywood siding (walls, door)
3	bundles, self-sealing asphalt shingles	5	bundles, self-sealing asphalt shingles
1	1x4 × 10' pine or fir door trim	1	1x4 × 10' pine or fir door trim
2	1x4 × 14' pine or fir door trim	2	1x4 × 14' pine or fir door trim
$1^1/_2$ lbs.	16d nails	2 lbs.	16d nails
1 lb.	8d nails	$1^1/_2$ lbs.	8d nails
$2^1/_2$ lbs.	8d spiral nails (flooring, roof)	3 lbs.	8d spiral nails (flooring, roof)
$2^1/_2$ lbs.	6d galvanized nails (siding)	3 lbs.	6d galvanized nails (siding)
$1^1/_2$ lbs.	$1^1/_2$" roofing nails	2 lbs.	$1^1/_2$" roofing nails

1 **Cutting and Assembling the Ribs.** The drawings on the facing page show rib details for 8- and 10-foot-wide sheds. Cut all the rib members to the lengths and angles shown in the drawing. Assemble the front-wall rib, rear-wall rib, and as many interior ribs as desired (three ribs for an 8-foot shed, four ribs for a 10-foot shed, etc.). Each rib is assembled on the ground, then lifted into position.

2 **Erecting the Ribs.** Cut two header joists to the length of the shed and mark the rib locations on

each. Have a helper hold each rib upright while you nail it to the header joists with two 16d galvanized nails. After you've installed all of the ribs, use a level to plumb them vertically, then tack 1×4 braces across the upper rib members to keep them in position. Remove the braces when you attach the sheathing.

3 **Installing the Flooring.** Use 6d nails to attach the plywood flooring to the joists; notch the panels, as shown on the drawing, to fit around the ribs.

4 **Adding Siding, Roofing, and Trim.** Attach the ½-inch plywood siding and waferboard or ply-

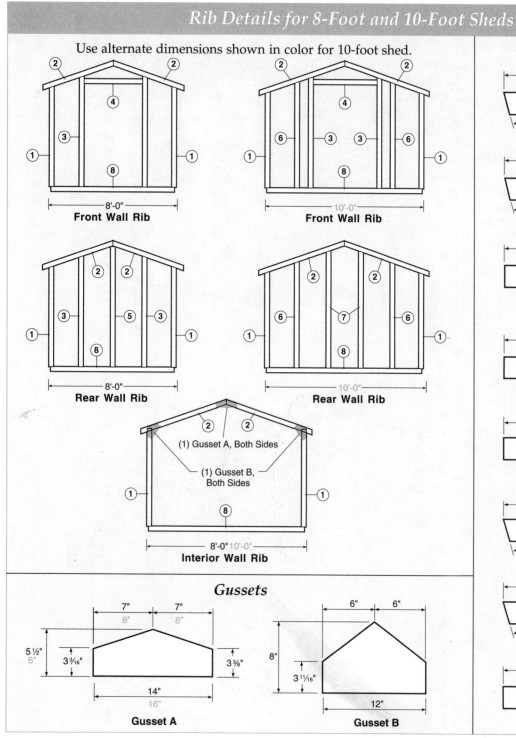

Use alternate dimensions shown in color for 10-foot shed.

Front Wall Rib — 8'-0"

Front Wall Rib — 10'-0"

Rear Wall Rib — 8'-0"

Rear Wall Rib — 10'-0"

Interior Wall Rib — 8'-0" 10'-0"

(1) Gusset A, Both Sides

(1) Gusset B, Both Sides

Gussets

Gusset A — 7" 7" / 8" 8", 5½" / 6", 3³⁄₁₆", 3⅜", 14" / 16"

Gusset B — 6" 6", 8", 3¹¹⁄₁₆", 12"

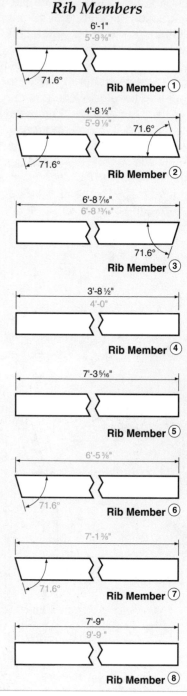

Rib Members

Rib Member ① — 6'-1" / 5'-9⅜", 71.6°

Rib Member ② — 4'-8½" / 5'-9⅛", 71.6°, 71.6°

Rib Member ③ — 6'-8⁷⁄₁₆" / 6'-8¹³⁄₁₆", 71.6°

Rib Member ④ — 3'-8½" / 4'-0"

Rib Member ⑤ — 7'-3⁵⁄₁₆"

Rib Member ⑥ — 6'-5⅜", 71.6°

Rib Member ⑦ — 7'-1⅜", 71.6°

Rib Member ⑧ — 7'-9" / 9'-9"

wood roof sheathing with 6d galvanized nails. Then attach the 1x4 corner trim, door trim, and fascia where shown in the drawing. Staple building felt on the roof sheathing and attach three-tab asphalt shingles with 4d roofing nails. For more on roofing and siding, see pages 60–68.

5 Building the Door. Make the door from the same material as the siding. Cut the door to provide ¹⁄₁₆-inch clearance on all sides between the door and the rough opening. Attach 1x4 door trim around the perimeter of the plywood door with screws or 3d galvanized finish nails

and construction adhesive, then cut pieces of 1x4 and attach them to form the "X" design shown on the drawing. Install 1x4 trim around the opening, as shown, then attach the door with sturdy hinges. For more on building doors, see page 71.

Barn-Style Shed

This barn-style shed uses simple rib construction. It consists of a front wall rib, a rear-wall rib, and as many interior ribs as desired for the shed length you want, spaced on 2-foot centers. Each interior rib consists of upper and lower roof chords (four total), two studs, plywood gussets, and a floor joist. Front- and rear-wall ribs include additional framing members as shown, and are made structurally stable by the plywood siding attached to them. The ribs are connected at the bottom with 2×4 header joists.

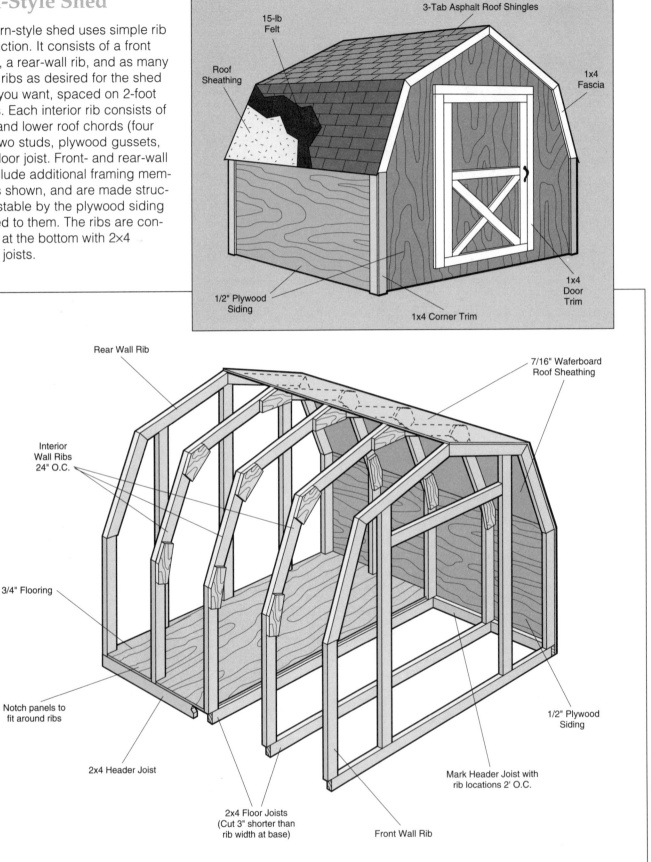

15-lb Felt

3-Tab Asphalt Roof Shingles

Roof Sheathing

1x4 Fascia

1/2" Plywood Siding

1x4 Corner Trim

1x4 Door Trim

Rear Wall Rib

7/16" Waferboard Roof Sheathing

Interior Wall Ribs 24" O.C.

3/4" Flooring

Notch panels to fit around ribs

2x4 Header Joist

2x4 Floor Joists (Cut 3" shorter than rib width at base)

Front Wall Rib

Mark Header Joist with rib locations 2' O.C.

1/2" Plywood Siding

Barn-Style Shed. Simple rib construction is used for this barn-style shed.

1 **Making the Rib Assemblies.** The drawings on the facing page show rib details for 8- and 10-foot-wide sheds. Cut all the rib members to the lengths and angles shown on the drawing. Assemble the front-wall rib, rear-wall rib, and as many interior ribs as desired (three ribs for an 8-foot shed, four ribs for a 10-foot shed, etc.). Assemble each rib on the ground, then lift it into position.

2 **Erecting the Ribs.** Cut two stringer joists to the length of the shed and mark the rib locations on each. Have a helper hold the ribs upright and plumb them while you connect them with temporary 1×4 braces (these will be removed later, as you install the siding). Once the ribs are aligned and plumb, nail the stringer joists to the rib-joist members with 16d nails.

3 **Installing the Flooring.** Use 6d nails to attach the plywood flooring to the joists; notch the panels, as shown in the drawing at the top of page 56, to fit around the ribs.

4 **Adding the Siding, Roofing, and Trim.** Attach the 1/2-inch plywood siding and waferboard or plywood roof sheathing with 6d galvanized nails. Then attach the 1×4 corner trim, door trim, and fascia where shown on the drawing. Staple building felt on the roof sheathing and attach 3-tab asphalt shingles with 4d roofing nails. For more on roofing and siding, see pages 60–68.

5 **Building the Door.** Make the barn-style door from the same material as the siding. Cut the door to provide a 1/16-inch clearance on all sides between the door and the rough opening. Attach 1×4 door trim around the perimeter of the plywood door with 3d galvanized nails, then cut pieces of 1×4 and attach them to form the "X" design shown on the drawing. Install 1×4 trim around the opening, as shown, then attach the door with sturdy hinges. For more on building doors, see page 71.

Materials List

8×8 SHED		10×10 SHED	
2	2×4 × 8' stringer joists	2	2×4 × 10' stringer joists
1	2×4 front-wall rib assembly	1	2×4 front-wall rib assembly
1	2×4 rear-wall rib assembly	1	2×4 rear-wall rib assembly
3	2×4 interior-wall rib assemblies	4	2×4 interior-wall rib assemblies
2	3/4" plywood sheets (flooring)	3½	3/4" plywood sheets (flooring)
4	7/16" waferboard sheets (roof sheathing)	5	7/16" waferboard sheets (roof sheathing)
1	1×4 × 8' pine or fir fascia/trim	1	1×4 × 8' pine or fir fascia/trim
6	1×4 × 12' pine or fir fascia/trim	6	1×4 × 12' pine or fir fascia/trim
6	1/2" plywood siding (walls, door)	7½	1/2" plywood siding (walls, door)
4	bundles, self-sealing asphalt shingles	5	bundles, self-sealing asphalt shingles
1	1×4 × 10' pine or fir door trim	1	1×4 × 10' pine or fir door trim
2	1×4 × 12' pine or fir door trim	2	1×4 × 12' pine or fir door trim
4 lbs.	2d nails (gussets)	4 lbs.	2d nails (gussets)
1/2 lb.	16d nails	1/2 lb.	16d nails
1/2 lb.	8d nails	1/2 lb.	8d nails
2½ lbs.	8d spiral nails (flooring, roofing)	3 lbs.	8d spiral nails (flooring, roofing)
2½ lbs.	6d galvanized nails (siding)	3 lbs.	6d galvanized nails (siding)
1½ lbs.	1½" roofing nails	2 lbs.	1½" roofing nails

Rib Members for 8-Foot and 10-Foot Sheds

Use alternate dimensions shown in color for 10-foot shed.

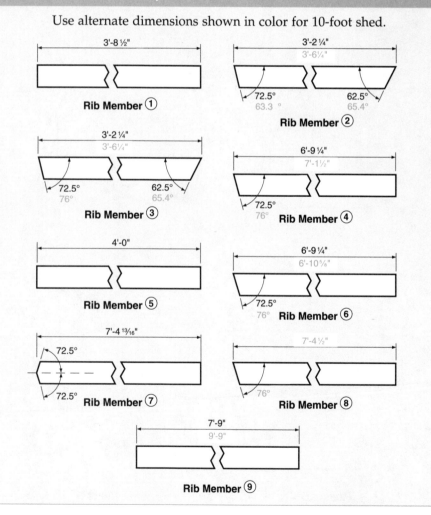

Use alternate dimensions shown in color for 10-foot shed.

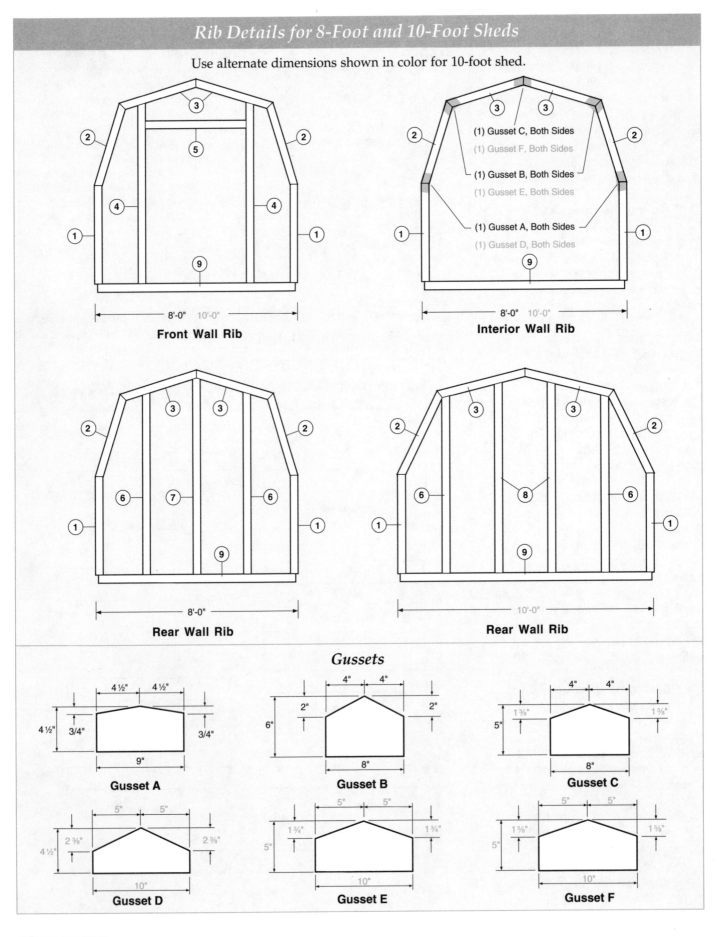

Front Wall Rib

8'-0" 10'-0"

Interior Wall Rib

(1) Gusset C, Both Sides
(1) Gusset F, Both Sides

(1) Gusset B, Both Sides
(1) Gusset E, Both Sides

(1) Gusset A, Both Sides
(1) Gusset D, Both Sides

8'-0" 10'-0"

Rear Wall Rib

8'-0"

Rear Wall Rib

10'-0"

Gussets

Gusset A
4 ½" 4 ½"
4 ½" 3/4" 3/4"
9"

Gusset B
4" 4"
2" 6" 2"
8"

Gusset C
4" 4"
1 ⅜" 5" 1 ⅜"
8"

Gusset D
5" 5"
2 ⅜" 4 ½" 2 ⅜"
10"

Gusset E
5" 5"
1 ¾" 5" 1 ¾"
10"

Gusset F
5" 5"
1 ⅝" 5" 1 ⅝"
10"

ROOFING & SIDING

Roofing and siding not only determine the finished appearance of the shed, but also protect it from the elements. This chapter shows how to install standard 3-tab asphalt shingles and several common types of siding.

Installing the Roof Deck

The roof deck, or sheathing, typically consists of $1/2$-inch plywood or $7/16$-inch waferboard. To assure a waterproof installation, cover the sheathing with 15-pound asphalt roofing felt. For roofs with a 4-in-12 pitch or steeper, a single layer of felt can be used, overlapping the edges by 2 inches. For lower-pitched roofs, apply a double layer of felt, overlapping each previous strip by one-half its width. Before applying the shingles, install drip-edge flashing at the eaves and gable ends, as shown at right.

1 Installing the Sheathing. Use 8d galvanized nails to attach the sheathing panels to the rafters. Place nails 6 inches apart around the panel edges, 12 inches apart where panels cross rafters. In most cases, the sheathing panels are applied with the long (8-foot) dimension running across the rafters. Stagger the panel ends so they don't all fall on the same rafter. Trim the sheathing flush with the eaves and rafter tails. At the ridge of a gable roof, extend the sheathing slightly past the ridge board. If you are installing fascia and soffits, do so before you attach the roofing felt. See page 76.

2 Installing Roofing Felt and Drip Edges. First, install the drip-edge flashing along the eaves, using 2d roofing nails spaced 8 to 10 inches apart. Next, use a heavy-duty staple gun and $1/2$-inch staples to attach the first felt strip along the bottom edge of the roof, allowing a $3/8$-inch overhang at the eaves. Attach successive strips, overlapping each by 2 inches (if single thickness) or by one-half the width of the strip (double thickness). If required, overlap strip ends by 4 inches. On gable or barn-style roofs, overlap the top strips of paper by 6 inches at the ridge, folding each one over and stapling it to the other side of the roof. Then install the drip-edge flashing at the gable ends (rake).

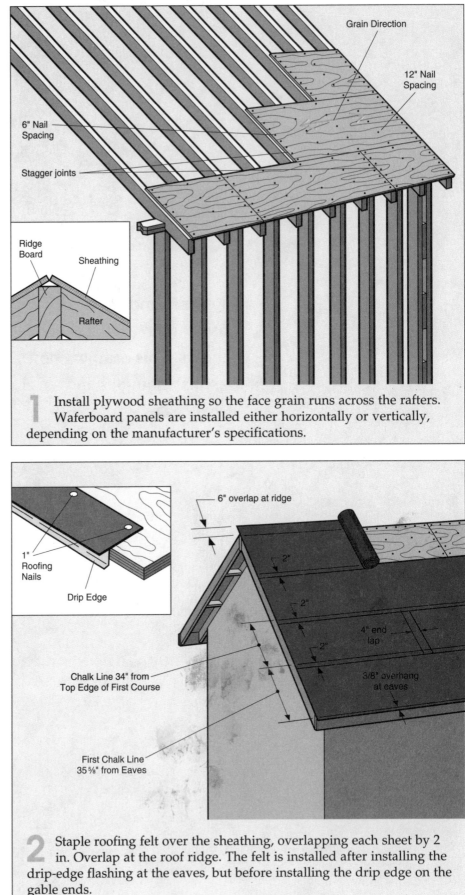

1 Install plywood sheathing so the face grain runs across the rafters. Waferboard panels are installed either horizontally or vertically, depending on the manufacturer's specifications.

2 Staple roofing felt over the sheathing, overlapping each sheet by 2 in. Overlap at the roof ridge. The felt is installed after installing the drip-edge flashing at the eaves, but before installing the drip edge on the gable ends.

Installing Three-Tab Asphalt Shingles

Before you start shingling, decide on a shingle pattern—that is, how the shingle tabs will be aligned. Three common patterns are centered, diagonal, and random alignment. For each pattern, start the first course with a full shingle. From there, each successive course involves removing a larger portion of the first shingle, then repeating with a full shingle, as shown in the drawing at right.

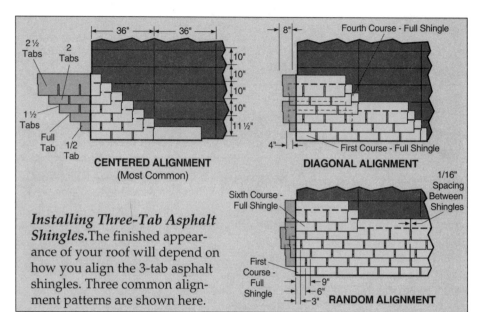

CENTERED ALIGNMENT
(Most Common)

DIAGONAL ALIGNMENT

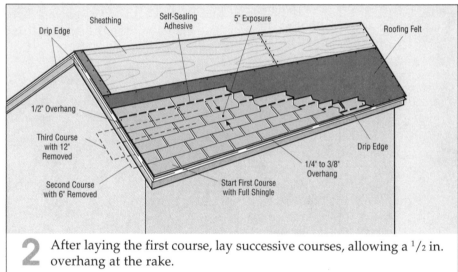

RANDOM ALIGNMENT

Installing Three-Tab Asphalt Shingles. The finished appearance of your roof will depend on how you align the 3-tab asphalt shingles. Three common alignment patterns are shown here.

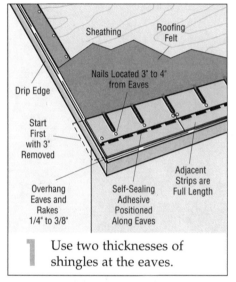

1 Use two thicknesses of shingles at the eaves.

2 After laying the first course, lay successive courses, allowing a ¹/₂ in. overhang at the rake.

1 At each eave, use two thicknesses of shingles. The first thickness, called a starter strip, is made of 12-inch-wide shingles installed upside down along the eaves lines. Remove 3 inches from the tab end of the first shingle in the course. Also remove 3 inches from one end of the first shingle in the starter course, as shown. Starter strips should overhang the eaves by ¹/₄ inch to ³/₈ inch. Attach each shingle with four 2d roofing nails.

2 Starting with a full shingle, lay the first course directly over the starter course. Align the first shingle so it projects about ¹/₂ inch over the rake and lies flush with the bottom edge of the starter course. Attach it with four roofing nails. When you reach the opposite end, cut the last shingle to provide a ¹/₂-inch overhang at the rake.

3 Using galvanized roofing nails, lay the remaining courses in the pattern you've chosen until you reach the ridge. Overlap shingles to provide a 5-inch exposure on the course beneath, or as given in the manufacturer's instructions. On roofs up to 10 feet long, you can usually align the shingles by eye; on longer roofs, use a set of horizontal chalklines, snapped every 2 feet across the roof, to serve as guidelines for aligning the courses. Install the last

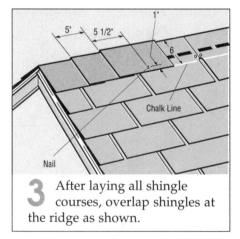

3 After laying all shingle courses, overlap shingles at the ridge as shown.

course on each side so that the shingles overlap the ridge; then install 7x12-inch ridge shingles as shown, or cut your own.

Siding

Popular types of siding include plywood, wood boards, hardboard, vinyl, and aluminum. Ideally, you would choose a siding that matches the house or other nearby buildings. Aesthetics aside, the least expensive choice is plywood.

Installing Wood-Board Siding

Wood-board siding comes in several species and in a variety of board widths and board "profiles," for horizontal, diagonal, or vertical application. Most have a 1-inch nominal thickness. Generally, wood is more expensive than other sidings, especially if you use a decay-resistant species, such as cedar or redwood. Because any wood is prone to decay, it requires frequent painting or staining. A stain containing a wood preservative/water repellent will extend the life of the wood.

Siding Types. Common horizontal sidings include clapboard, bevel, and various styles of channel siding. Board-and-batten and board-on-board sidings are installed vertically. Shiplap, channel, and tongue-and-groove sidings can be installed horizontally or vertically.

Application. Because there are so many types of board sidings, we can't provide specific installation instructions for all of them. The drawing below shows nailing details for the types of siding just mentioned. Nominal 1-inch siding boards are attached with 8d or 10d galvanized finishing nails; use smaller nail sizes for thinner boards and battens. Predrill nail holes at board ends to prevent splitting.

You can nail horizontal siding directly over studs, but the wall framing should be reinforced with 1×4 diagonal bracing (recessed, or "let in," to the studs on the inside of the wall), as shown on page 37. Vertical siding will also require diagonal bracing, as well as horizontal nailing blocks between the studs, or cleats attached to them every 2 feet to provide a nailing surface for the boards. In both cases, staple a layer of building paper or felt to the studs before you apply the siding, for extra weather protection. Sheathing generally isn't required under most board sidings, but check local codes to be sure.

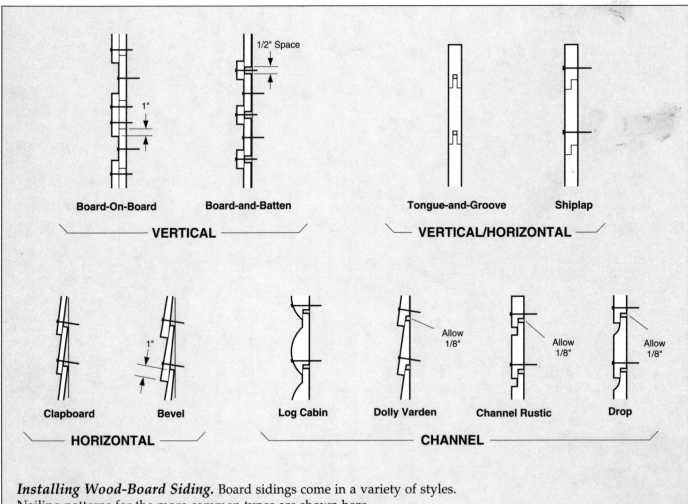

Installing Wood-Board Siding. Board sidings come in a variety of styles. Nailing patterns for the more common types are shown here.

Installing Plywood Siding

Plywood siding comes in several surface textures, in 4-by-8- and 4-by-10-foot sheets. It is the most economical siding you can install, especially because it also serves as the wall sheathing and can be attached directly to the studs with no additional bracing. Panels are usually installed vertically; if you install them horizontally, blocking between the studs will be required where the panel edges meet.

1 Positioning the Panels.
Choose a panel length (8-foot or 10-foot) that is long enough to extend several inches below the level of the inside floor. If you have a poured-concrete perimeter foundation or concrete slab, the siding should extend slightly below the top of the foundation, as shown at left below. Make sure the bottom of the siding is at least 3 inches above ground level, however. Depending on the roof design, you may want to notch the panel to fit around rafters under the eaves. To provide additional weather protection, staple building paper or felt over the studs before installing the siding.

2 Installing the First Panel.
Strike a level chalk line across the mudsill or header joist as a guide for aligning the bottom edges of the plywood panels. At one corner of the building, install the first panel, using 6d galvanized nails spaced 6 inches apart along the panel edges and 12 inches apart where the sheet crosses studs. Carefully align one side of the panel flush with the corner of the building, and the other side on the center of a stud. Be sure the inside edge is perfectly plumb; if it isn't, the out-of-plumb condition will worsen progressively as you install adjacent panels. Use a level to check for plumb.

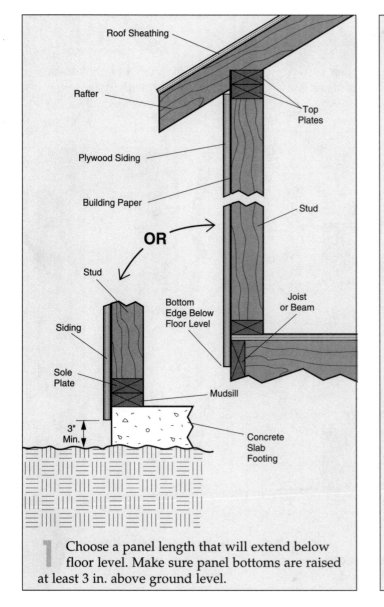

Roof Sheathing

Rafter

Plywood Siding

Building Paper

OR

Stud

Top Plates

Stud

Joist or Beam

Stud

Siding

Sole Plate

Bottom Edge Below Floor Level

Mudsill

3" Min.

Concrete Slab Footing

1 Choose a panel length that will extend below floor level. Make sure panel bottoms are raised at least 3 in. above ground level.

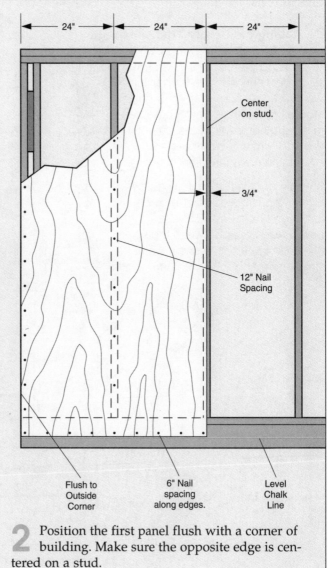

24"   24"   24"

Center on stud.

3/4"

12" Nail Spacing

Flush to Outside Corner

6" Nail spacing along edges.

Level Chalk Line

2 Position the first panel flush with a corner of building. Make sure the opposite edge is centered on a stud.

3 Installing the Remaining Panels.
Install successive panels, leaving a 1/16-inch expansion gap between each one. The gap can be either caulked or covered with a vertical wood batten, as shown here.

4 Installing Doors and Windows.
When you reach the rough opening for a door or window, you can avoid creating extra panel joints by simply nailing the full panel(s) over the opening, then making a cutout from inside the shed, as shown at top right. Start cuts at each corner with a drill and keyhole saw or portable jigsaw, then finish up with a hand saw. If the window is already installed, leave a 3/8-inch gap between the plywood and window frame, and fill with caulk.

5 Adding the Corner Trim.
When you come to a corner, position the plywood panels as shown, caulk the corner, and add the corner trim. Two trim options are depicted here. Caulk all remaining joints where panels meet other parts of the building, then add trim around doors and windows if you have installed them.

To apply panels horizontally, follow the same basic steps but provide blocking at horizontal joints, as shown. Add caulk between the upper and lower panels to prevent water from penetrating the joint, then cover with a thin wood batten.

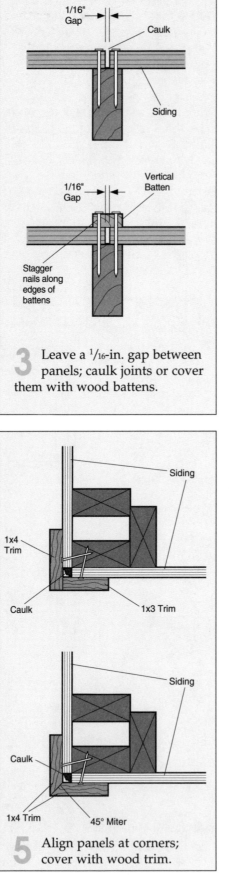

3 Leave a 1/16-in. gap between panels; caulk joints or cover them with wood battens.

5 Align panels at corners; cover with wood trim.

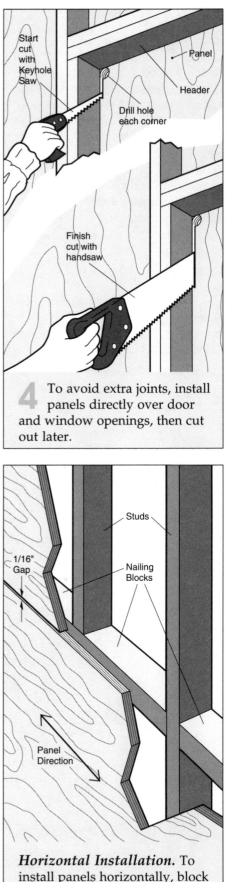

4 To avoid extra joints, install panels directly over door and window openings, then cut out later.

Horizontal Installation. To install panels horizontally, block between studs at panel joints.

Installing Hardboard Siding

Most hardboard siding simulates horizontal board lap sidings, with or without a wood-grain texture. The "boards" are typically 9 to 12 inches wide by 12 feet long. You also can buy channel siding boards that are applied either horizontally or vertically, and 4×8 panels with a simulated wood-grain or stucco texture.

Hardboard sidings come unfinished, primed, prestained, or prepainted in a limited variety of pastel colors, usually whites, grays, and earth tones. The prepainted finish carries a limited guarantee against color fading, the period depending on the quality you buy. Prestained sidings simulate natural wood tones, but the finish doesn't last as long as that of prepainted sid-

ings. Primed sidings are less expensive than prestained or prepainted ones and are a logical option if you want to paint the shed a color of your choice. Unfinished sidings require both priming and painting.

The siding material itself usually carries a 25-year warranty against denting, cracking, and deflection. However, it is susceptible to rot and termite damage if not installed properly.

Most hardboard siding manufacturers offer various accessories, such as color-matched nails and caulk, as well as color-matched molding for inside and outside corners, J-moldings, drip caps for window openings, and Z-flashing for panel joints.

1 Installing the Sheathing and Furring. Hardboard lap siding should never be installed directly

over studs, or the panels will become wavy. Use 3/8-inch plywood or waferboard for sheathing, covered with building paper or felt.

In wet climates, you may need to install furring strips between the sheathing and siding to allow a breathing space in order to prevent damage from moisture condensation inside the walls. The strips must be at least 1/4 inch thick. For horizontal siding, install the furring strips vertically, over the studs. For vertical siding, install the furring horizontally. For diagonal siding, install the furring diagonally in the opposite direction. Insect screen is installed between the furring strips and the bottom plate to keep bugs from getting in the wall space. Check local codes and instructions that come with the siding you've chosen to see if furring strips are required.

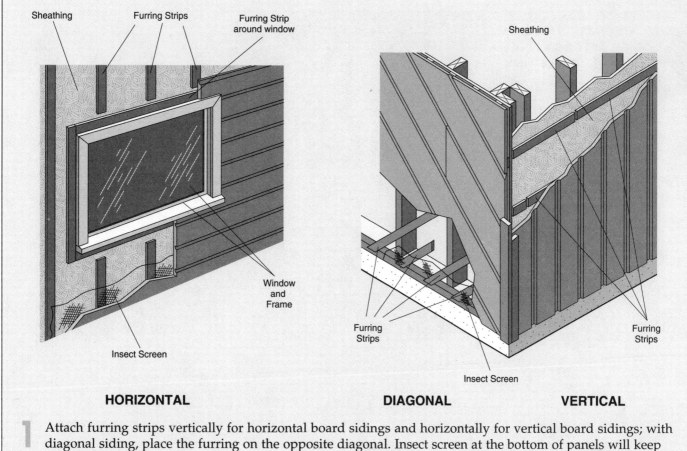

HORIZONTAL   **DIAGONAL**   **VERTICAL**

1 Attach furring strips vertically for horizontal board sidings and horizontally for vertical board sidings; with diagonal siding, place the furring on the opposite diagonal. Insect screen at the bottom of panels will keep insects out of the wall cavity.

2 **Nailing the Paneling.** Nail the siding to the wall at stud locations, using 6d galvanized spiral nails or nails recommended by the siding manufacturer. Again, note that some manufacturers offer color-matched nails for prepainted panels and lap siding. Always join panel or board ends over studs or furring strips; also, stagger the joints so they don't align with each other.

The cut ends of panels or lap siding should be painted or treated with a water repellent. Allow at least a 1/8-inch gap between adjacent panels or boards and corner, window, and door trims.

3 **Adding Caulk and Trim.** Fill gaps with flexible caulk. Special metal moldings and flashing are available for finishing inside and outside corners, and to cover exposed panel or board edges to provide a more finished appearance.

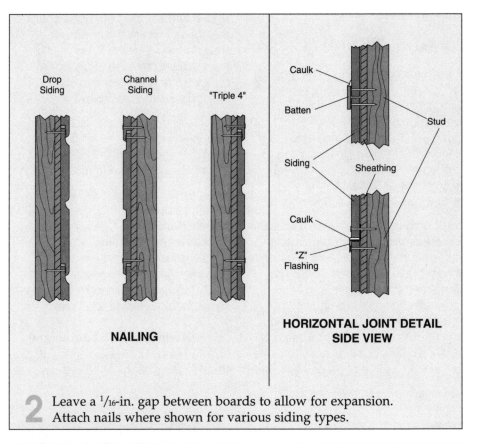

2 Leave a 1/16-in. gap between boards to allow for expansion. Attach nails where shown for various siding types.

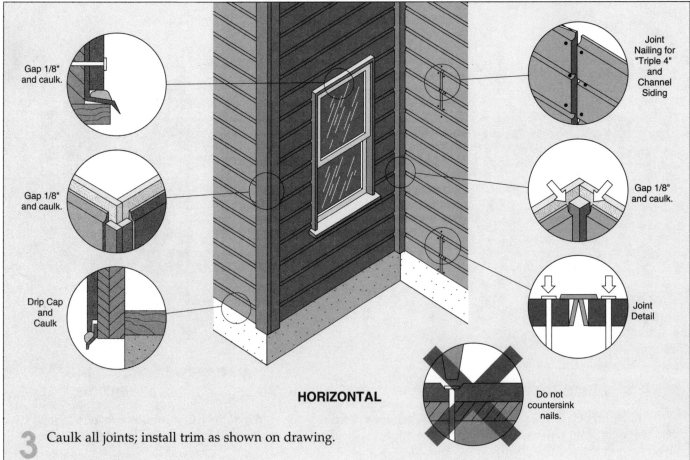

3 Caulk all joints; install trim as shown on drawing.

Installing Vinyl Siding

Like hardboard siding, vinyl siding simulates wood-board sidings. It's not quite as realistic-looking as hardboard, but because the color runs completely through the siding material, vinyl siding never needs painting. Board styles include horizontal lap sidings, and channel sidings for vertical or horizontal application. Siding panels are approximately 8 to 10 inches wide by 12 feet long; each panel simulates one or more boards. Colors are generally limited to whites, grays, light pastels, and earth tones, although a few darker solid colors are available from some manufacturers.

Vinyl siding packages include assorted trim strips and channel moldings required for installation, starter strips, inside and outside corners, fascia, soffit panels and trim, and window and door trim. These trim pieces serve to hold the panels in place, and provide a finished, uniform appearance. Vinyl gutters and downspouts are available in colors to match the siding.

Common tools needed to install vinyl include hammer, tape measure, aviation shears, utility knife, worktable, and ladders or scaffolding. Special tools include nail-slot punch, snap-lock punch, zip tool, and scoring knife; these should be available where you buy the siding.

Most home centers and lumberyards sell vinyl siding and trim pieces as a package, which includes easy-to-follow step-by-step instructions. On this and the next page, we will review the general installation procedure.

1 **Nailing the Panels.** When installing siding and trim pieces, use galvanized roofing nails or nails recommended by the siding manufacturer. The nails should have a smooth shank and a flat head. When nailing the panels and trim, place nails in the center of the pre-punched nailing slots unless otherwise indicated. Do not nail panels tightly or the siding will buckle in hot weather.

2 **Cutting the Panels.** The easiest way to cross-cut panels to length is with aviation shears. To cut panels lengthwise, score along the cut-line with a utility knife, then bend the panel back and forth to snap it. Corner posts and trim strips should be cut with a hacksaw because shears will crush the channel.

3 **Installing the Corner Posts and Starter Strips.** Whether you're installing panels horizontally or vertically, you must attach the corner posts, starter strips, and trim accessories before the panels are fitted and nailed in place. Allow a 1/4-inch space where trim accessories meet and at panel ends where they fit into the trim accessories.

First, determine the starting point of the siding at the bottom of the shed wall. Then snap a horizontal chalk line at the bottom of the wall between the two corners of the building to create a level baseline.

Install the corner posts at the four outside corners of the shed, then install the starter strip. Note that you may need to install a plywood furring strip behind the starter strip in order to make a uniform plane for the siding panels.

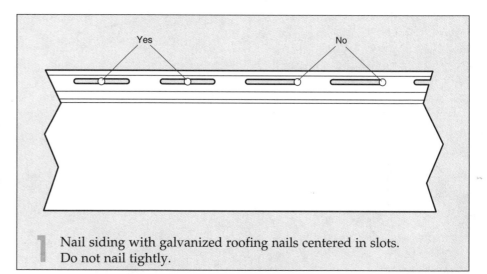

1 Nail siding with galvanized roofing nails centered in slots. Do not nail tightly.

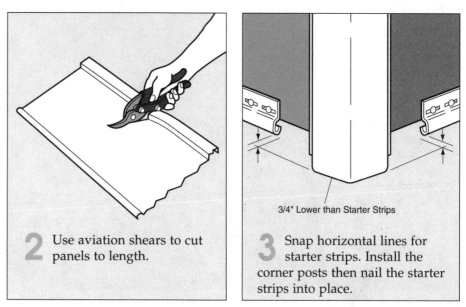

2 Use aviation shears to cut panels to length.

3 Snap horizontal lines for starter strips. Install the corner posts then nail the starter strips into place.

4 **Installing the Window and Door Trim.** Next, trim the doors and windows according to the manufacturer's instructions. The type of trim required will depend on whether the siding is installed vertically or horizontally. This drawing shows trim for horizontal siding. Finally, install the trim under the eaves and gable rakes. For horizontal siding, undersill trim is used at these locations; for vertical siding, use J-channel trim.

5 **Attaching the Panels.** After you've installed all the trim pieces, lock the first panel into the starter strip. Allow ¼ inch of space at the end of the panel within the cavity of the corner post. Then install successive panels until you've covered the wall. Where panel ends meet, overlap the ends by 1 inch, with all laps going in the same direction. When overlapping panels, cut off about 1½ inch of the nailing flange from the end of one panel to allow for expansion. Run the overlaps away from the most common focal point of each wall, such as away from each side of the front and rear entries to the house. Offset the joints by at least 24 inches so that they don't form a continuous vertical seam.

After the siding is installed, use an acrylic latex or silicone caulk (preferably the same color as the siding) to caulk all joints prone to water penetration, including spots where pipes or wires penetrate the wall, and within the J-channel on the sides of windows and doors. Caulking is not recommended between the panels and other trim strips or between the panels themselves.

6 **Installing the Soffits and Fascia.** Use perforated soffit panels if you will be ventilating the attic through the eaves. Otherwise use smooth surface soffit panels. If you're installing vinyl soffits and fascia, refer to the manufacturer's instructions for specific details. You can also install a wood fascia and soffit to the rafter ends and at the eaves, as described on page 76.

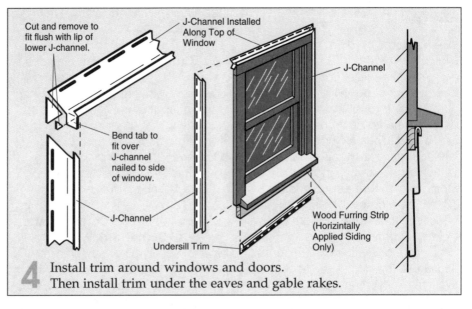

Cut and remove to fit flush with lip of lower J-channel.

J-Channel Installed Along Top of Window

J-Channel

Bend tab to fit over J-channel nailed to side of window.

J-Channel

Undersill Trim

Wood Furring Strip (Horizintally Applied Siding Only)

4 Install trim around windows and doors. Then install trim under the eaves and gable rakes.

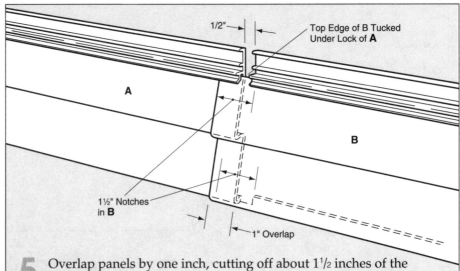

1/2"

Top Edge of B Tucked Under Lock of A

A

B

1½" Notches in B

1" Overlap

5 Overlap panels by one inch, cutting off about 1½ inches of the nailing flange from the end of the panel to allow for expansion.

Perforated Soffit Panel   **Smooth Soffit Panel**

6 Use perforated soffit panels if you will be ventilating through the eaves. Otherwise use smooth soffit panels.

FINISH WORK

This section shows how to make your own door or install a prehung factory-made door, make and install windows, build enclosed soffits, and install gutters and downspouts. It also provides options for shelving.

Installing a Prehung Door

Prehung exterior doors come complete with top and side jamb pieces, stops, and in some cases, thresholds. They're typically attached to the jamb assembly and held in place with shipping braces. Doors and jamb components are also available separately. Factory-made doors are typically 6 feet, 8 inches tall, and come in a variety of widths, from 2 feet to 3 feet. Double doors are also available. Most prehung doors come with complete installation instructions, including the rough opening size.

Installation Sequence. If the shed will have plywood or board siding attached directly to the studs, attach the siding first, then position the door jamb in the opening with the outside edge flush to the outside face of the siding. If you're installing board siding over sheathing, install the door frame after you do the sheathing, but before the siding. Position the door frame so that it projects past the sheathing by a distance equal to the siding thickness. Then run siding up to the edges of the door jamb, and install trim as shown at bottom right.

1 **Setting the Door in Place.** If the door comes with an attached jamb, keep the shipping braces intact. Place the unit in the opening so that it will swing in the desired direction. Exterior doors usually swing inward, although on small sheds you may want the door to swing outward to maximize storage space. Remove the shipping braces, then check the clearance between the top of the door and the head jamb: it should be a uniform 1/8 inch. If the space at the top on the lock side is too great, shim under the hinge jamb to raise the door.

2 **Attaching the Hinge Jamb.** Use a level to plumb the hinge jamb on the face and edge, then insert shims behind the jamb at the points to be nailed. Adjust the shims to provide a uniform clearance between the jamb and the rough opening. If the jamb is twisted, insert two nails side by side through the jamb to correct the problem. Nail the jamb in three places from top to bottom.

3 **Attaching the Lock Jamb and Head Jamb.** Before nailing the lock jamb and head jamb, recheck the tolerances; the space should be a uniform 1/8 inch between the jamb and the door. If the lock side is too tight, shim under the lock jamb to correct the situation. Plumb, shim, and nail the lock jamb to the rough opening as you did the hinge jamb, then shim and nail the head jamb at the center to prevent sag.

4 **Attaching the Trim.** When the jamb is nailed in place, attach the door trim as shown in the drawings at right, below. Paint the door, jamb, and trim, then install the lockset per the manufacturer's instructions.

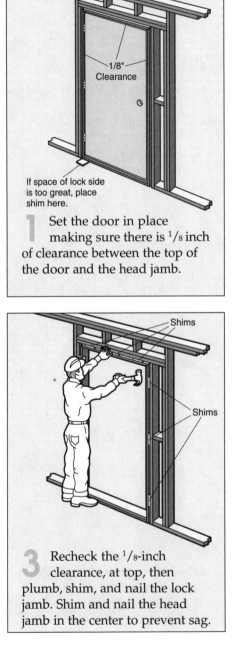

1 Set the door in place making sure there is 1/8 inch of clearance between the top of the door and the head jamb.

1/8" Clearance

If space of lock side is too great, place shim here.

3 Recheck the 1/8-inch clearance, at top, then plumb, shim, and nail the lock jamb. Shim and nail the head jamb in the center to prevent sag.

Shims

Shims

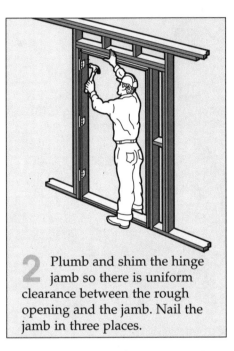

2 Plumb and shim the hinge jamb so there is uniform clearance between the rough opening and the jamb. Nail the jamb in three places.

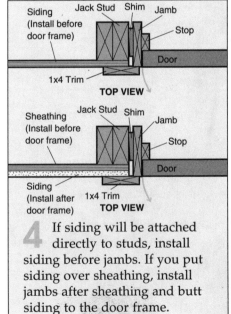

Siding (Install before door frame)   Jack Stud   Shim   Jamb
Stop
Door
1x4 Trim
TOP VIEW

Sheathing (Install before door frame)   Jack Stud   Shim   Jamb
Stop
Door
Siding (Install after door frame)   1x4 Trim
TOP VIEW

4 If siding will be attached directly to studs, install siding before jambs. If you put siding over sheathing, install jambs after sheathing and butt siding to the door frame.

Making Your Own Door

If you need a door to fit an odd-size opening, or simply want to save money, you can easily build your own door from plywood and 1x4s, or wood boards. Some possibilities are shown below. Doors up to 3 feet wide by 6 feet, 8 inches tall can be made of ³/₈- to ⁵/₈-inch plywood (or plywood siding), reinforced with

1×4s. The same 1-by stock can be used to make the trim to frame the rough opening. Because the door will be installed with surface-mounted hinges, no jamb is needed. For taller or wider doors, use plywood-covered 2×4s for the door frame, or make a solid Z-frame door from 1×6s or 1×8s, as shown on the drawing. If the opening is over 4 feet wide, it's usually better to install double doors; a single door will be too heavy.

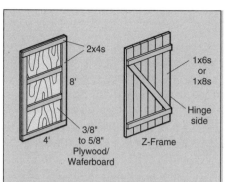

Making Your Own Door. Large doors can be made with plywood and 2×4s or with a Z-frame of 1×6s or 1×8s.

Making a Plywood Door

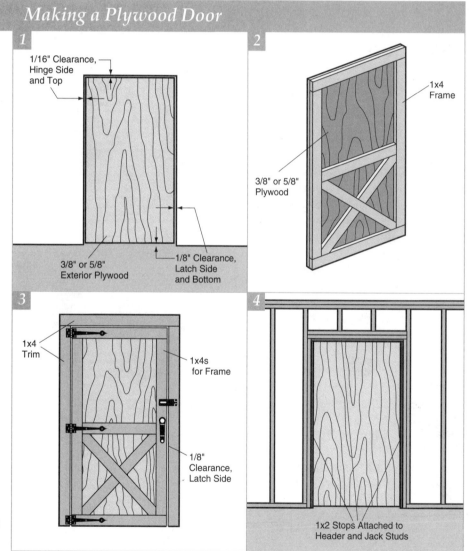

1. Cutting the Door to Size. Measure the rough opening size, then cut a piece of plywood to provide ¹/₁₆-inch clearance at the hinge side and top of the opening, and ¹/₈-inch clearance at the latch side and door bottom.

2. Adding 1×4s. Cut 1×4 pieces to length and attach them around the perimeter of the plywood as shown on the drawing. The pieces can be attached with short galvanized screws or with small galvanized finish nails and construction adhesive. If you are using long strap hinges, such as those shown in the drawing, center another 1×4 across the face of the door. The X made of 1×4s on the lower door panel provides additional reinforcement and improves the appearance of the door.

3. Hanging the Door. A variety of hinge and latch styles are available for hanging exterior doors; surface-mounted butt hinges, strap hinges, and T-hinges (shown) are most common. When attaching hinges, use screws long enough to reach through the trim and siding and into the wall studs. Make sure the hinges are large enough to support the weight of the door. Hinges and other door hardware should be galvanized or otherwise rust resistant.

4. Attaching the Door Stops. Close the door, then install 1×2 stops directly to the header and jack studs inside the rough opening. If you're

installing double doors, you'll also need to install a doorstop across the bottom of the opening.

Installing Windows

Decide whether you want a fixed-pane or operable window. You can make your own fixed-pane window as shown on the facing page. Two common types of operable windows are wood-sash windows (either double-hung, like the one shown, or casement windows, which open outward like a door) and aluminum sliding windows.

Windows usually come with specific installation instructions, including the rough opening size. Whether you install the window before or after the siding depends on both the window and the siding you've chosen.

Making the Rough Opening. If you are framing a rough opening for a used window you've picked up, make the opening about ¾-inch wider and longer than the window's frame. This will allow room for squaring the window.

Installing Windows with Casing. Some windows come with an exterior casing or "brick molding" on the outside. Install the window from the outside, nailing through the brick molding into the outside of the framing. In some models you take the sash out and nail through the jambs into the sides of the framing. In any case, shim the windows plumb and level before nailing as shown in the drawing at bottom right.

Installing Windows with Nailing Flanges. Some windows, including aluminum windows and windows made of vinyl-clad wood, come with a nailing flange around the outside. Nail these windows to the outside of the framing. Depending on the look you want to achieve, you can cover the flange with casing and bring the siding to the casing, or cover the flange with siding, using no casing at all.

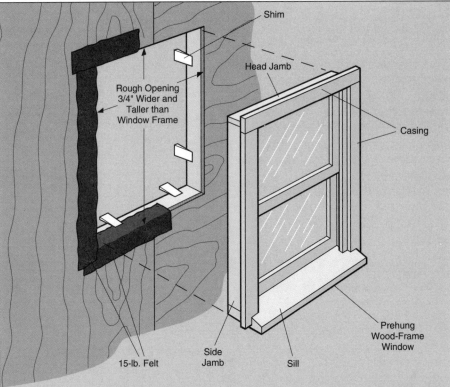

Installing Windows with Casing. If you are installing windows that have casing, nail the casing to the framing and install the siding so that it butts the casing.

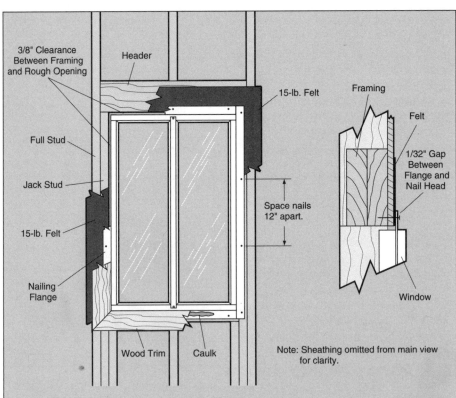

Installing Windows with Nail Flanges. If you are installing windows that have nailing flanges, nail the flanges to the framing and cover the flanges with casing or siding.

Making Your Own Window

You can easily make a wood-frame, fixed-glass window to fit into a rough opening of any size, fashioning the individual frame components yourself and installing them piece by piece. As shown on the drawing at right, the basic frame members include a head jamb, two side jambs, and a sill. Face stops and backstops, which hold the glass in place, can be square or quarter-round stock. Buy the window glass and have it cut to exact size at a glass shop or hardware store. The following instructions can be adapted to suit your particular requirements.

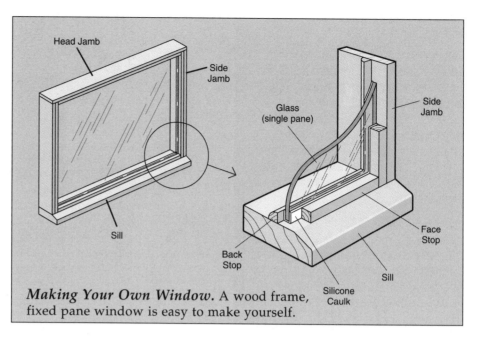

Making Your Own Window. A wood frame, fixed pane window is easy to make yourself.

1 Cut the sill and jamb pieces to length and install them in the rough opening. Note how the outside top edge of the sill is beveled for water runoff. Bevel-cut the sill on a tablesaw or with a hand plane, or have the work done at a cabinet shop. Use a framing square and level to make sure the frame members are perfectly square and level within the opening. If necessary, drive shims between the window framing and wall framing to square the opening. Attach the sill with 8d casing nails and the jamb members with 6d casing nails.

2 Measure the inside height and width of the window opening, then cut a piece of glass $1/8$ inch shorter and narrower than these dimensions. Use 2d casing nails to attach the backstops in the desired position within the window frame.

Run a heavy bead of silicone caulk around the window frame against the backstop.

3 Put the glass against the backstop, pushing around the edges until the caulk oozes out. Apply more caulk if needed, then nail the face stops in place with 2d casing nails, being careful not to angle the nails into the glass. Install trim as desired.

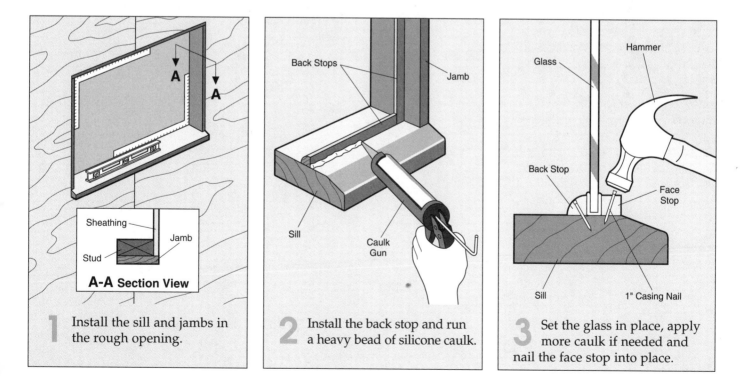

1 Install the sill and jambs in the rough opening.

2 Install the back stop and run a heavy bead of silicone caulk.

3 Set the glass in place, apply more caulk if needed and nail the face stop into place.

Gutters & Downspouts

Many home improvement centers and lumberyards offer a choice of aluminum or vinyl rain-carrying systems, which include gutters, downspouts, and related installation hardware. If you've installed vinyl or aluminum siding, you probably will choose a system of the same material in a matching color. If you have another type of siding, you can use either material and in the color of your choice.

Aluminum gutters come in a variety of colors and are lightweight, making them easy to handle. Their baked enamel finish eliminates the need for painting, although you can repaint them to match your trim. Aluminum is corrosion resistant, but it does dent more easily than vinyl. The components are assembled with aluminum connectors, and the joints are caulked to prevent leaks.

Vinyl gutters are also lightweight, easy to handle, and virtually maintenance free, but the colors are limited and vinyl is not easily repainted. Although most vinyl systems must be welded together with solvent, some have self-sealing, snap-together components for easier installation.

The drawing below shows the basic components of a typical rain-carrying system. The actual appearance of the parts will vary from one type to another. The gutter is mounted to the fascia with brackets, hidden hooks, or spikes and ferrules. Optional accessories include leaf guards, downspout strainers, downspout diverters (to direct water away from the foundation), and rafter brackets (for roofs without fascia boards).

Following are some general tips for installing these systems. Use them in conjunction with the manufacturer's instructions.

1 **Installing the Gutter.** The gutter should be spaced on 24- to 30-inch centers, or as specified by the manufacturer. Make sure the gutter has a slight slope from the high end to the drop outlet for the downspout (approximately 1/4 inch of drop per 10 feet of run). Attach a guide string at the high end of the fascia, about 3/4 inch below the overhanging roof shingles, as shown on the facing page. At the low end, use a level to make the string horizontal, and then drop the string slightly to provide the required slope. The edge of the shingles should extend about 1/2 inch past the inside edge of the gutter. If the shingles extend too far over the gutter, it will be hard to clean. If necessary, shim out the gutter by attaching spacer blocks behind the gutter brackets.

Use the string as a guide to attach the gutter brackets or hooks—the string represents the top edge of the

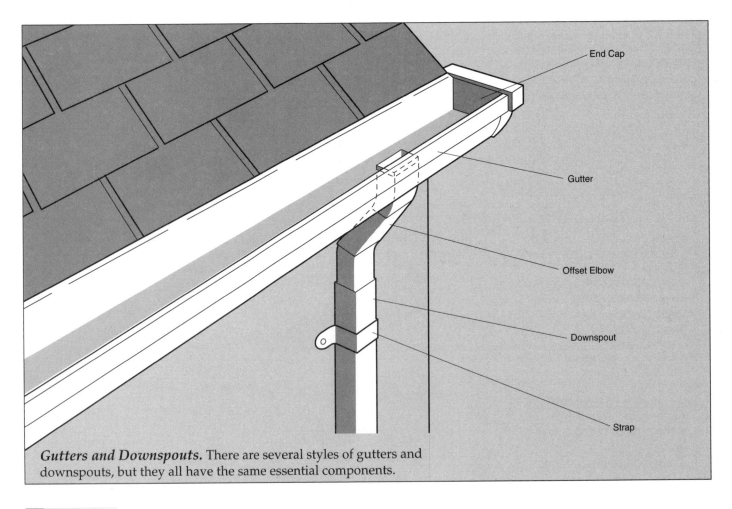

Gutters and Downspouts. There are several styles of gutters and downspouts, but they all have the same essential components.

End Cap

Gutter

Offset Elbow

Downspout

Strap

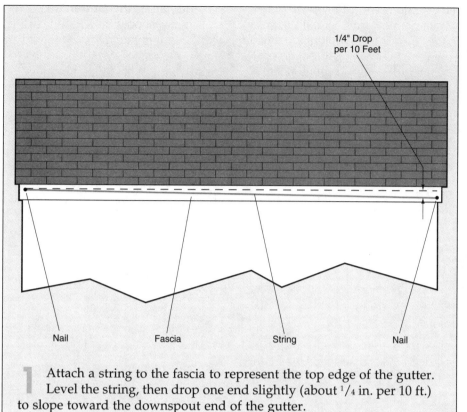

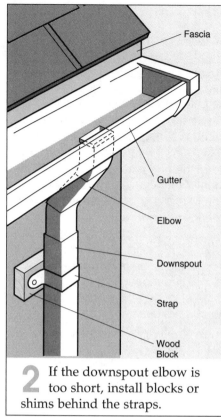

1 Attach a string to the fascia to represent the top edge of the gutter. Level the string, then drop one end slightly (about $^1/_4$ in. per 10 ft.) to slope toward the downspout end of the gutter.

2 If the downspout elbow is too short, install blocks or shims behind the straps.

gutter. Sections of vinyl or aluminum gutter can be cut to length with a hacksaw.

2 Installing the Downspout. After installing the gutter sections and drop outlet, connect the downspout to the drop outlet with two elbows and a short length of downspout to form an offset. The downspout is attached to the wall with the straps provided. Place wood blocks or spacers behind the straps to shim out the downspout if necessary, as shown at top right.

3 Installing the Diverter. At the bottom of the downspout, you'll need to provide a means of diverting the water away from the foundation and preventing soil erosion and puddles. One method is to place a concrete or plastic splash block beneath the downspout. Or, you can used a hinged diverter fitting. A short length of downspout is attached to the bottom end of the fitting, which can be swung upward to accommodate lawn cutting.

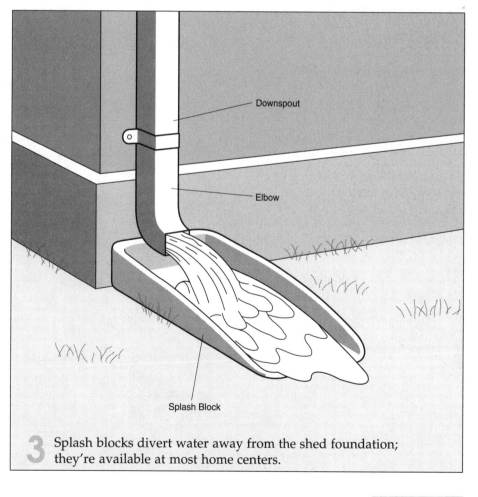

3 Splash blocks divert water away from the shed foundation; they're available at most home centers.

Finishing Touches

Once you've finished building the basic shed and have installed the doors and windows, apply any remaining trim. You can use 1×4s or 1×6s around doors and windows, axnd 1×6s as fascia nailed across the rafter ends. On gable and barn-style roofs, the fascia can extend up along the end rafters at the gable ends. You can use 1×2 vertical battens, spaced 8 to 12 inches apart on exterior plywood walls, to give the shed a rustic board-and-batten look. A 1×6 or 1×8 skirt board can be used around the base of the shed to hide exposed foundation members (beams, joists, and so on). Trim at the corners usually consists of a 1×3 and 1×4, arranged as shown in the inset drawing at right. This arrangement makes both trim strips look equal in width and is simpler than making a mitered corner with two 1×4s to achieve the same effect.

Horizontal or Sloping Soffit

For a more finished look, you can enclose the eaves with a horizontal or sloping soffit, as shown at lower right. Soffit material can be 3/8-inch or 1/2-inch exterior A/C plywood. Once you've added the desired trim, use a good quality caulk to seal any remaining joints on the shed exterior.

For a horizontal soffit, add a cleat and lookouts at each end as shown. Attach the plywood soffit. Make the fascia wide enough to overhang the soffit by about 1/2 inch. Install 1×2 trim.

For a sloping soffit, nail plywood directly to the bottom of the rafters.

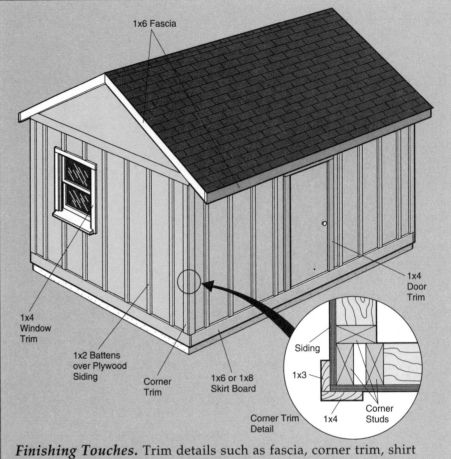

Finishing Touches. Trim details such as fascia, corner trim, shirt boards, and battens make your shed attractive and durable.

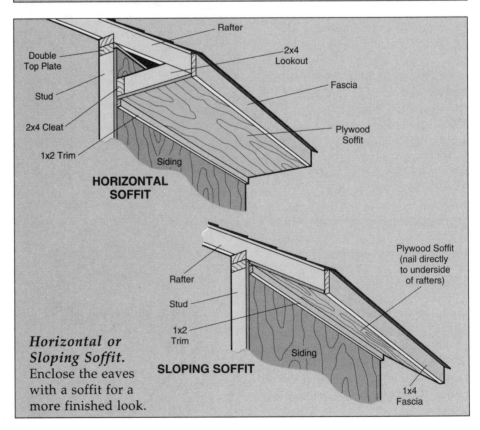

Horizontal or Sloping Soffit. Enclose the eaves with a soffit for a more finished look.

Painting Tips

If you want to paint the shed, select a premium-grade exterior latex or alkyd paint. Latex paints are water-based, odorless, quick to dry, and easy to clean up. Alkyd paints, inaccurately referred to as "oil-based," are slow-drying and require mineral spirts for thinning and cleanup.

Transparent and semitransparent stains are two other options. Transparent stains color the wood but allow the natural grain pattern and some of the natural wood color show through. Semitransparent stains mask the wood color and grain pattern, but are thinner than paint, so much of the wood texture is visible. Stains generally don't provide as much protection as paints and need to be reapplied more frequently. To increase the life of the building, choose a stain with a wood preservative and water repellent.

Whichever paint or stain you choose, apply at least two coats. New wood should be primed with a good-quality latex or alkyd primer before painting. If you choose to leave the shed unfinished, at least apply a clear wood preservative or preservative and water sealer.

Preparing the Surface

The most important factor in any painting job is a well-prepared surface. For paint or stain to adhere properly, it must be applied to a clean, dry surface—free of dirt, dust, and grease. For a professional-looking job, fill all dents, cracks, and holes with exterior spackle or wood putty, then sand smooth. Also sand any rough spots on exterior trims and moldings.

Painting Tools

In addition to the painting tools discussed here, you'll need a roller extension, roller tray, stepladder, paddles for stirring paint, dropcloths, and masking tape. Instead of a paint pan for rolling, you can use a special grid designed to fit inside a 5-gallon paintbucket. Also consider a roll of plastic sheeting or plastic dropcloths to cover nearby plantings, especially if using a spray gun.

Brushes. Brushes are made with either natural or synthetic bristles. Natural bristles should never be used with water-based (latex) paints and stains; the bristles absorb water and become clogged. When shopping for brushes of any size, check the following points: The handle should be comfortable and easy to clean. The brush should feel full when gripped around the bristles. The bristles should be flagged (split) and fanned slightly; good bristles do not clump when pressed against your palm, and spring back into position afterward. Tug the bristles; reject the brush if they come loose. For most exterior painting, you'll need two brushes: a thick, 3-inch or 4-inch brush for large areas, and a 1½-inch or 2-inch angled sash brush for cutting in around windows.

Rollers. Roller covers vary in thickness and the composition of the nap. The rougher the surface you'll paint, the thicker the roller nap should be. Most roller covers are nylon; more expensive ones are lamb's wool. Buy the best roller cover you can afford; cheap ones wear out quickly, apply paint unevenly, and are generally frustrating to use. Most roller frame handles are threaded to accept an extension handle. Extension handles may be wood or aluminum and range from 2 feet to 10 feet in length; some aluminum ones are telescopic.

Pads. Painting pads are easy to use, fast, and versatile. Different sizes are available for painting corners, trimming and cutting in, and painting large areas. Some are designed for use with rough surfaces, such as rough-sawn plywood siding.

Sprayers. On large sheds, using a sprayer may save time—either a compressed-air or airless model. Both types generate considerable overspray and require careful masking of windows and other surfaces to protect them from paint. Wear a respirator and safety glasses when using either type.

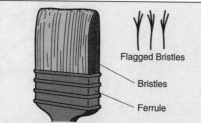

Brushes. Bristle ends should be flagged to hold paint. The ferrule should be solidly attached, the handle comfortable.

Pads. Paint pads my be used for flat surfaces as well as trim. Extension poles attach to threaded sockets.

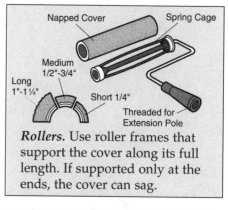

Rollers. Use roller frames that support the cover along its full length. If supported only at the ends, the cover can sag.

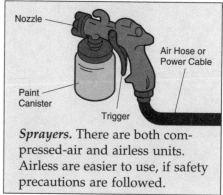

Sprayers. There are both compressed-air and airless units. Airless are easier to use, if safety precautions are followed.

Storage Ideas

Once your shed is finished, you'll probably want to outfit it with shelves, hooks, racks, and other means of maximizing storage space. This page shows several methods of attaching shelving to the interior walls, along with other storage ideas.

Shelf Brackets. The easiest way to install sturdy shelving is to use shelf brackets. These can be installed directly to the wall studs. Three common types include angle brackets, continuous shelf brackets, and adjustable shelf brackets. Continuous shelf brackets are made of galvanized steel shaped into a continuous Z pattern, and hold up to three shelves. They're relatively inexpensive and will accommodate shelves up to 12 inches wide. Attach them directly to the wall studs with flat-

head wood screws, then attach the shelves to the brackets with shorter wood screws. Adjustable shelf brackets consist of a vertical slotted channel with individual steel brackets that hook into the channel anywhere along its length. The channels are attached vertically to the wall studs with screws. You then position the brackets where desired. The brackets come in various lengths to support shelves of different widths. The shelves simply sit on top of the brackets. Simple angle brackets (made of galvanized steel) are fastened to the studs with screws; the shelves are attached to the bracket with screws from underneath.

Pegboard. This familiar, versatile storage system consists of tempered hardboard perforated with evenly spaced holes, which accept a wide variety of hooks and hangers. You

insert the hooks into the holes where desired. Pegboard comes in several thicknesses (typically 1/8 inch and 3/16 inch), and various panel sizes (4x4, 2x8, and 4x8). Installing pegboard, space it from the wall so that the hooks can be inserted into the holes. One option is to attach 1x2s around the perimeter with screws; another is to use spacers between the pegboard and screws. You can attach the pegboard in this manner to studs or a solid wall. Make sure you attach the screws at stud locations.

Simple Workbench. If the shed will double as a workshop, you can make a small, freestanding workbench such as the one pictured below, with a cutting list for its components. The workbench can be removed from the shed if you need additional storage space.

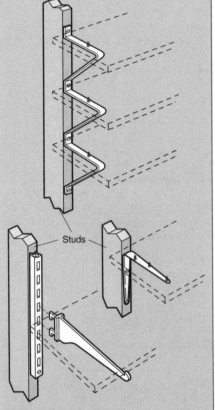

Shelf Brackets. Common shelving supports include (tiop to bottom) continuous (Z) brackets, slotted-channel brackets, and angle brackets.

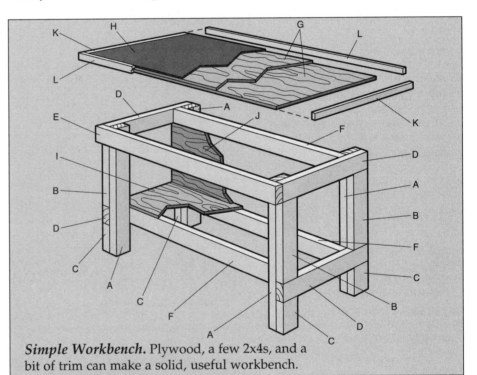

Simple Workbench. Plywood, a few 2x4s, and a bit of trim can make a solid, useful workbench.

Cutting List

A	4	2x4 x 28 1/2" legs
B	4	2x4 x 15 1/2" top leg cleats
C	4	2x4 x 6" bottom leg cleats
D	4	2x4x 20 1/2" crossbraces
E	1	2x4 x 46" leg brace (front, top)
F	3	2x4 x 43" leg braces
G	2	24" x 48" 3/4" plywood top

H	1	24" x 48" 1/4" hardboard top
I	1	13 1/2" x 46" 1/2" plywood shelf
J	1	15" x 46" 1/2" plywood backstop
K	2	1x2 x 24" trim strips (benchtop)
L	2	1x2 x 49 1/2" trim strips (benchtop)

Backfill Earth, sand, or gravel used to fill the excavated space under a foundation.

Battens Narrow boards used to cover joints in plywood or board siding.

Batter Boards Temporary structures that hold strings used to locate and square the corners of a building.

Bird Blocking Short wooden blocks placed between rafters above the top plate to keep out birds and small animals. Screened holes in the blocking, called soffit vents, provide ventilation.

Bird's-Mouth Cut A cutout in a rafter where it crosses the top plate of the wall, providing a bearing surface for nailing. Also called a heel cut.

Blocking Short pieces of lumber installed between framing members, to reinforce the framing or provide a nailing surface for panel edges or board ends.

Bridging Metal struts or 1x2s placed in an X pattern between floor joists to keep them from twisting or warping.

Chalk Line String or cord covered with chalk; snapped against wood members to mark for measurement or cutting.

Cleat A short length of wood fastened to a joist, wall stud, or other framing member to support horizontal framing pieces, shelves, and other components.

Collar Tie A horizontal cleat placed between rafters to prevent them from pushing the walls outward and to prevent them from sagging at midspan.

Course A single continuous row of surfacing or building units, such as shingles, bricks, or tiles.

Cripple In wall framing, a short vertical member placed between header and top plate at openings; also used to support sills beneath windows.

Dry Well A gravel-filled hole used to receive and drain water runoff; part of a drainage system to which water runoff is directed via a perforated drainpipe.

Fascia Wood trim applied to rafter tails at eaves or to end rafters on the gable end of a building.

Footing The widened, below-ground portion of a poured concrete foundation or foundation wall, or a poured concrete base on which precast concrete piers are placed.

Frost Heave Shifting or upheaval of the ground due to alternate freezing and thawing of water in the soil.

Frost Line The maximum depth to which soil freezes in winter; your local building department can provide information on frost-line depths in your area.

Gable The triangular portion at the end walls of a gable-roof structure; gable roofs consist of two equal pitches that form a peak at the building centerline.

Grade The ground level. "On grade" means at or on the natural ground level.

Gusset A piece of plywood used to reinforce a framing joint, typically in roof-truss construction.

Head Jamb The top member of a door or window frame; on doors, the frame consists of a head jamb, two side jambs, and a threshold; window frames are the same, except the bottom member is called a sill or stool.

Header A horizontal framing member placed across the top of an opening to support the structure above.

Header Joist A joist attached across the ends of the floor joists at the perimeter of the building.

Jack Stud A partial stud nailed next to full studs to support the header at door openings. Also called a trimmer.

Joist A structural member placed perpendicular to beams in floor framing.

Ledger A horizontal board attached to an existing structure to which joists or rafters for an attached shed or other structure, such as a deck are affixed.

Mudsill A wood foundation member bolted to a concrete slab or foundation and on which other framing members can be placed; mudsills are usually pressure-treated 2x4s or 2x6s.

Outrigger A short block notched into the end rafters on gable roofs to support sheathing at the roof overhang.

Pier A precast concrete block set on or into the ground to support wood foundation members, such as posts, beams, girders, or joists.

Platform Framing A framing method that involves building a plywood floor platform on which the walls are erected. Less common is "balloon framing," in which the wall studs extend below floor level, where they are attached directly to the mudsill.

Rib A preassembled framing unit that includes a set of roof-framing components (for example, a roof truss), wall studs, and sometimes a floor joist. The ribs are erected on 16- or 24-inch cen-

ters and tied together with roof sheathing and siding. Typically used for smaller prefabricated sheds and barns.

Ridge Board A framing member at the roof peak to which opposing rafters are attached.

Run and Rise In rafter layout for gable roofs, the horizontal and vertical measurements used to determine roof pitch. The values are expressed as a ratio; if the rafter rises 4 inches for every 12 inches of run, it is said to have a 4-in-12 pitch. The total run equals one-half the total span (see Span, below); the total rise is the distance from the top plate to the rafter centerline at the roof peak.

Sheathing Panels or boards attached to exterior walls or roofs to provide a nailing surface for roofing and siding materials.

Skirt Board A trim piece or band (usually a 1x6, 1x8, or 1x10 board) placed at the bottom of a wall, below the siding, to hide substructure members such as joists and beams.

Stringer Joist A joist attached to the ends of header joists and lying parallel to the floor joists.

Sole Plate In wall framing, the bottom plate to which the studs are attached.

Span The distance between vertical supports for horizontal framing members, such as joists or beams. For rafters or trusses, the span is the distance between the two opposite walls that support them.

Stud Anchor A headless threaded fastener with an expandable tip, inserted into a hole drilled in a concrete footing or foundation. The projecting threaded end makes it possible to attach a ledger by means of a nut and washer.

Top Plate In wall framing, the top horizontal framing member to which the studs are attached; typically, the top plate consists of doubled 2x4s, which are overlapped at the building corners to form an interlocking joint.

Truss A preassembled framing unit made up of several individual framing members, such as ceiling joists, rafters, and associated bracing. Joists are reinforced with plywood gussets or metal nailing plates.

Variance A formal waiver from a municipal building department or similar agency to allow an exception to local codes or ordinances on some nonconforming feature of a building project.